Feisty

Feisty

Chronicles & Confessions of an Old PR Warhorse

Joe Finnigan

THE BALLAD OF IRA HAYES
Written by Peter LaFarge
Used by permission of Edward B. Marks Music Co.

ISBN-13: 9781540705662
ISBN-10: 1540705668
Library of Congress Control Number: 2016919868
CreateSpace Independent Publishing Platform
North Charleston, South Carolina

Passage on Pages 94 & 95 used with permission of Jim Morice

Back cover author photo by Jack MacDonough

To Connie and the kids with love

Introduction

For many years, family members, friends, colleagues, and clients alike urged me to write a book. This book.

For the longest time I demurred, using the admittedly contrived and convenient excuse that too many of those who'd be part of the story are still alive and too many of the escapades too recent. But times change. People and organizations move on, are swallowed up, or implode, and people do die. Besides, frankly, as time passed I'd come to regard so many other books by public relations people or about the business as either unduly unctuous, unnecessarily theoretical, inconsequential, or dull. Nevertheless, some may feel this violates the semisacred code of *omerta* that prevailed in our business. Hopefully a statute of limitations factor of sorts has ameliorated that sensitivity. And anyone inclined to quibble over the revelations is welcome to weigh the personal ones against the others.

When finally I did decide to embark on this project, I jokingly told those who knew about it and more or less favored the idea that for $10,000 they could be in the book, or for $20,000 I'd leave them out.

The encouragement to write no doubt was inspired by an abundance of rich and eventful professional and personal experiences, including ten-plus full-throttle, turbocharged years as lead spokesman and communications counsel for Anheuser-Busch during arguably, at least to that point in time, the most tumultuous post-Prohibition period in the storied brewery's existence, followed by significant client relationships with a number of other major corporations and their top executives. As such, there is a generous serving of what might be termed "inside baseball." And if the style seems a bit too journalistic, sorry, perhaps my DNA is showing.

What's ultimately emerged, for better or worse, are the details—impressions and memories of real people and events. As such, it's part memoir and part time capsule—straightforward, richly anecdotal, and for cathartic purposes, seasoned with an occasional dollop of venom. Hopefully it provides, from one key player's perspective, an authentic glimpse of what life was like first in a more or less embryonic public relations agency and later in one that attained the highest echelons of its industry globally, plus a sense of the associated personal glories attained and human costs exacted. Highly intimate, it includes numerous mettle-testing, bizarre, and almost spiritual twists and turns seen through the alternately triumphant and tormented eyes of someone known for creativity; a rough-and-tumble, no-holds-barred operating style; an acerbic tongue; an aversion to fools and phonies; and an obsession to get things done—frequently paying dividends for self, family, clients, and colleagues while at other times wreaking havoc on those same lives and relationships.

As much as anything, however, it's about the public relations business—an up-close look at life in the PR fast lane and how it was (and still is) practiced, in some cases on almost a daily basis, and fate. It spans parts of five decades, beginning in the late 1960s, and covers an era that saw major changes in society as well as advances in communications, how business is conducted, and how personal and institutional values are formed, although granted many of those advances have been obliterated by the ongoing tech-social media revolution. It deals too in a sense with the notions of risk taking, self-reliance (sometimes to a fault), and facing up to one's vulnerabilities played out as part of an organization that, thanks to an almost perfectly aligned combination of unbridled collective entrepreneurship, raw talent, enormous energy, and savvy leadership, became an international communications consulting juggernaut. Along the way, while there was no magic involved, we pulled lots of rabbits out of lots of hats—benefiting clients as well as ourselves.

Finally, for thirty-five years in the PR business, nearly thirty of them with Fleishman-Hillard, possibly the best full-service agency in the world, during good times and others, with triumphs and setbacks, it was an honor, a point of pride, and more often than not, a pure, unadulterated blast!

—JTF, Saint Louis, Missouri 2017

Note: This is a memoir, a true story, based on my best recollections of various events and life experiences. All of the people named are real and their roles true. Some are cited for the roles they played but are not named; that is to protect their identities and/or me from embarrassment or allegations of defamation.

Book One

One

Saint Louis, Missouri—it was Christmas morning, 1997. I was in the bathroom shaving. All I had on was a towel, and KMOX, the mighty 50,000-watt AM radio station, which was airing a holiday tradition—the annual three-hour live broadcast from the home of the late Jack Buck, one of the best radio sports play-by-play announcers (and wits) ever to grace the airwaves. Over the years the Christmas show had become the thing to tune in to and the place to be heard from for a veritable *who's who* of local sports, political, and business figures. It was interrupted by only a few commercials and a Christmas carol or two with vocals by whomever happened to be there at the time, the melodies supplied by the Bucks' favorite cocktail lounge piano virtuoso. "Before we go any further this morning," Buck interjected, "I want to extend warm regards to our friend Joe Finnigan. He's retiring after nearly thirty years as a mainstay with Fleishman-Hillard, the powerhouse public relations agency, and we wish him the very best." I was caught completely off guard, but was naturally flattered, by those kind remarks; within the next couple of hours the phone rang off the hook at our house as friends, neighbors, and clients who'd been listening called with their felicitations.

• • •

It began inconspicuously enough fifty-three years earlier on a day that historically was anything but, a quick one hundred miles north of here in the Illinois capital city of Springfield. It was Saturday, August 26, 1944—the very day General Charles DeGaulle, out of exile, triumphantly strode the 1.9 kilometer length of the Champs-Elysees in observance of the Allied Forces' liberation of Paris as two million Frenchmen lining the avenue celebrated deliriously.

My father, twenty-nine-year-old Army Infantry First Lieutenant Joseph Thomas Finnigan, did not live to see that day. He was a World War II combat casualty; after just four days in battle a victim of the horrific carnage in the Normandy hedgerows, a month and two days after the D-Day invasion and six weeks to the day before I arrived. Word of his death reached my mother, the former Mary Frances McCarthy, on August 2, her twenty-ninth birthday, in the form of the most dreaded of deliveries, a yellow War Department telegram with four stars on the envelope and the frigid greeting, "We regret to inform you..." They had been married for only a year when it happened. Eventually, after much prayer and agonizing, she elected to have her husband permanently interred at the American Cemetery at Omaha Beach (Colleville-sur-Mer), hoping to avoid a family split over whether to bury his remains in Springfield or Saint Louis, where he grew up and, for the most part, his family still lived.

When Lt. Finnigan (330th Regiment, 83rd Infantry) left Camp Breckenridge, Kentucky, for Europe, Mary Frances returned to her hometown of Springfield to give birth, moving in with her parents and seven younger brothers and sisters. Then, as a war widow, she began raising me in the old family residence—an imposing white American Foursquare house skirted by a wraparound front porch, almost a landmark on the corner of bustling South Grand Avenue West and Whittier Street. With eleven regular inhabitants, all but one of them adults, it was easy to be overlooked; the place was notorious for its nonstop, Irish Catholic, booze-fueled chaos: music, laughter, profanity, arguments, and brawls amid a perpetual procession of friends, relatives, and suitors. At the time the mayhem seemed quite normal to me, as did the adults' proclivity for secrecy—to talk in code about touchy situations when younger ears were nearby, to always appear proper and dignified, and to keep tears out of sight, genuine troubles bottled up.

For decades, Mary Frances's father, Dr. David Henry McCarthy, practiced medicine, delivering hundreds of babies and caring for many of the movers and shakers in Sangamon County, a locale with plenty of both. He'd worked his way through medical school in Chicago early in the twentieth century, briefly doing duty side-by-side with Sister Frances Cabrini, the first US citizen to be a canonized saint by the Catholic Church. He seemingly was never home, being either at his office, at the hospital, or making house calls. He drove a big green Packard and was extremely hard of hearing, so everyone in the household tended to be loud, and he smoked foul-smelling, cheap Dutch Masters cigars. I called him Daddy because that's what his daughters called him—besides, I didn't know any better.

Mary Frances's mother, Ella Giblin McCarthy, was a classic post-Victorian lady. Educated (as was Mary Frances) by convent nuns, Ella was a trained concert flutist, accomplished enough to perform with the Chicago Philharmonic. She was soft and round, had blue-gray hair, and her sons called her Chubbo, which she hated. However, her constitution was anything but; Ella was as tough and fearless as she was refined. Raising four girls and four rambunctious boys almost on her own, she had to be. For that reason I'd much rather have disobeyed my mother than Nana, as she was known, because she was far more strict and quick to dole out punishment. Ella and her firstborn also were inveterate naggers, which explains my lifelong aversion to browbeating. At the same time, she and Mary Frances were deeply religious women who managed adversity by making marathon prayer novenas and offering it up for the poor souls in purgatory, whatever the difficulty faced. Never mind that to this day I'm not sure where purgatory is, what it is, or if it really exists.

"The loss of a loved one is beyond man's repairing."—World War II Secretary of War Henry Stimson. The quote is from Rick Atkinson's *The Guns at Last Light: The War in Western Europe, 1944–1945.*

Growing up in Springfield, I did not know my father's family nearly as well. I understood, however, that Townsend W. Finnigan, my paternal grandfather, never got over the loss of his son Joe. He hailed from Monroe City, a rural canker of twenty-five hundred souls, two hours north of Saint Louis and seventeen clicks west of Hannibal, Missouri. His family of origin was almost as rowdy as the McCarthy clan, a distinction cinched when his brother, Chester, died of injuries he sustained in a bar fight. By contrast Towny, as he was known, was smart, dapper, and going places.

As a young man he migrated south to the big city to seek his fortune. He married Cora, one of the Buckman girls of Monroe, and went to work at the stockyards in East Saint Louis, across the Mississippi in Illinois, eventually becoming a partner in Woodson, Fennewald, a brokerage firm that made a market in hogs and other livestock. T. W., as he also was known, did well enough to own a four-hundred-acre farm outside Monroe City, worked by tenant help.

The Finnigans made the trek often to the farm from their fine red-brick duplex at the corner of Spring and Utah Streets in South Saint Louis. Joseph Thomas, the youngest of Towny's four children and only son, became interested in the agriculture business at an early age, and with a career in that field in mind he enrolled in Saint Louis University's School of Commerce. He'd earlier graduated from the university's Jesuit-run college prep where he excelled academically and starred in tennis. Unfortunately, as America's involvement in World War II loomed, he found himself in the army before fully realizing his career aspirations. He and Mary Frances met during her sole semester in Saint Louis at Fontbonne College, after which she transferred to Chicago's Northwestern University, graduating in 1937 from the renowned Medill School of Journalism.

Mary Frances was beautiful, talented, and ambitious. Upon returning to Springfield as an expectant mother she resumed her journalism career, taking on dual reporting jobs with a local radio station and *The State Register*, back then the afternoon newspaper. Her *Society Page of the Air* program was heard each morning on WCBS-AM, then Springfield's top station, and her newspaper beat mirrored her radio work. She was a stickler for good manners and proper English usage—constantly drilling me on pronouns, plurals, possessives, the works. So my comportment and command of the language, forced as they sometimes may have been, were considered remarkable at an early age. By age three or four I could recite "The Owl and the Pussy Cat" in its entirety with near perfect inflection to the apparent delight of those I deigned favor with a rendition of Edward Lear's classic nonsensical verse. Perhaps that and a lifetime of writing and editing account for an occasionally insufferable compulsion to correct the spoken and written blunders of others—like I'm infallible.

Reeling from her grief, Mary Frances was loathe to allow me out of her sight. I was the one genetic link to her lost love, and she went to exceptional lengths to paint a vivid, glowing picture of the father I'd never know. "Your daddy was a great guy and a war hero," she'd say while showing me an article from the local newspaper that called him one. (Years later I realized it was an obituary.) She would trot out pictures of the late lieutenant as well as the personal effects the War Department returned to her in his footlocker—his dress cap, infantry ring, Purple Heart, wristwatch, fountain pen, the American flag that adorned his casket, and other belongings. Yet he wasn't necessarily a hero to me; all I understood was that he wasn't there. I felt different—at home, the only child in the midst of the confusion and fussiness of the surrounding adults, and otherwise not like the other kids my age. It was painful; I just didn't know how much so at the time. But clearly I was different from the others—a "war orphan," an outsider of sorts, disconnected from and envious of those whose fathers were with them and whose mothers and other family members were not quite so pampering and possessive. Amid the hovering, at some emotional depth, I felt a gnawing sense of loss—cheated, less than, inadequate, and over time turned bitter, resentful, and, truth be told, afraid. Photos indicated a strong physical resemblance between father and son. I could see that. Still there was this nagging, irrational, and unspoken question whether the all-too-brief wartime union of Mary Frances and Lt. Finnigan ended in an abandonment of sorts. As time passed I coped with it more or less, but not always successfully, with compartmentalization—usually by trying to ignore his memory or pretend he never existed, even though he always lurked in a remote corner of my consciousness. After all, as I would come to discover, ancestry—knowing who we are and where we come from—is one of life's most powerful forces. It would take more than forty years and a trip to France before I could fully come to terms with the reality, irrigate the emotional scar tissue, and properly acknowledge, mourn for, and make amends to my departed namesake. In the intervening years, those feelings became hardwired in, combining to leave me fending for myself emotionally—symptomatically self-reliant, cynical, and somewhat distrustful of others. Vestiges of those traits endure to this day.

I listened often to my mother's daily radio program on the family's Philco upright. I was too young to understand what the show was all about, but I liked hearing her voice, especially her usual farewell: "For WCBS and the Society Page of the Air, thanks for listening. This is Mary Frances Finnigan. Good-bye. Joey, I love you, and I'll see you soon." I loved the attention, and thus exposed, was captivated by broadcasting at an early age. I took great delight in the children's programs, dramas, and comedies of the day—shows like *Big John and Sparky, The Lone Ranger, Gangbusters, Sergeant Preston of the Yukon, Fibber McGee & Molly*, and *The Great Gildersleeve.* I also listened to newscasts presented in those postwar days by pioneering legends like Murrow, Lowell Thomas, Kaltenborn, Heatter, Severeid, and others. When the family acquired its first television set a few years later, also a Philco, I was almost as smitten by the 1954 Army-McCarthy and Kefauver hearings and by Chet Huntley and David Brinkley's coverage of the rambunctious political conventions of the 1950s as by the top TV kids' shows of the day—*Captain Video and His Video Rangers, The Pinky Lee Show, Howdy Doody*, and *Sky King.*

(In the late 1940s, CBS bought the B, paying the owners of WCBS a reported $1 million for the letter. It enabled the network to have WCBS as the call letters for its New York flagship; the Springfield station thus became WCVS and remains so to this day.)

Two

When I was six, my mother remarried. My stepfather, another World War II veteran named John Gregory McFall, was a senior official with the Federal Housing Administration office in Springfield—a bureaucrat. Mary Frances rationalized the union on at least two counts: that I needed a father figure, a male influence, plus she insisted that the silver-maned, debonair McFall was one of the town's most elegant and eligible fellows in his bachelor days and was still a good catch some years later. Eight years her senior, he was tardy for everything, but eventually he would arrive all Brooks-Brothered-up, wafting a faint but unmistakable aspect of witch hazel and talc. After the wedding we moved into a modest two-bedroom, one bath bungalow on South Douglas Avenue in southwest Springfield.

As an Irish Catholic Republican, Greg McFall was somewhat of an anomaly, which in time I came to find curiously fascinating since the rest of my maternal family of origin was solidly and unquestioningly Democratic. He was fresh from a first marriage of his own that ended tragically with the suicide of his young bride. (Word was that the first Mrs. McFall, a nurse named Vera who hailed from the small nearby town of Taylorville, reportedly had numerous gentlemen callers while Greg was overseas serving as an officer in the army's Quartermaster Corps in the Persian Gulf Command.) His consequent anger and an affinity for Beefeater gin made him a stern taskmaster and, at times, insufferably domineering—occasionally even scary. He'd come home occasionally loaded for bear, as the saying goes, and we'd try to steer clear of him lest we get the brunt of his scorn either in the form of verbal put-downs or, on other occasions, the back of his hand. Yet even though he and Mary Frances had a child of their own together, a son they named John Gregory Jr., he seemed to take a genuine interest in me and had a decided influence on my views and values, which would be increasingly evident later in life—attitudes toward work, relationships, politics, and the like. He even offered to adopt me legally, but Mom wisely tabled that idea for fear it would confuse me and dishonor the memory of my biological father. Nevertheless, adaptable and eager for a father of my own, I came to accept and appreciate Greg McFall, including eventually even calling him Dad.

Mom stayed home after remarrying and worked to make ends meet. She clipped coupons, saved S&H Green Stamps to get things for the home, and entered contests left and right—with frequent although modest success. She'd inherited a Baldwin parlor grand piano, which she played rather well, but it was too big for our small bungalow, so she negotiated to trade it in for a brand-new Betsy Ross Spinet, which fit nicely. She saved every one of the government checks she got as a result of my dad's World War II death, so when it came time for me to go to college there was money for that, and after graduating my stepdad, Greg McFall, by then my legal guardian, turned over to me a tidy sum that remained.

Three

At age five or six I was entrusted to the Ursuline nuns, a branch of strict German educators who staffed the K-8 Blessed Sacrament parish grade school. Besides the usual—reading, writing, and 'rithmetic—the good sisters, being good sisters, espoused the "other big three," faith, hope, and charity, plus two other virtues: self-control and something they called gumption. By the time I was in fifth or sixth grade it was clear that, as the emerging class clown and smart ass, I exhibited an acute shortage of them all and was usually in some kind of trouble. Acting out, it's called today, and from very early on I was rebellious, a real handful. Such behavior prompted David, the eldest of my mother's four brothers, to dub me Malarky, a nickname that stuck for a number of years. Yet notably by age twelve I'd wake by 5:00 a.m., hop on my green-and-white fat-tire Schwinn, deliver eighty copies of the *Chicago Tribune* to neighborhood homes, and arrive at the Church of the Blessed Sacrament in time to serve 6:30 a.m. mass. In those days altar boys were still servers—no girls allowed, the liturgy still in Latin, and the priests kept their hands to themselves.

The nuns were confounded; clearly they saw that I had the brains, verbal proficiency, and a strong, albeit willful, personality to do well, but these were offset by lackluster scholarship and certain chronic behavioral deficiencies. Only our family's relationship with the pastor kept me in school long enough to graduate. At about the same time my mother was diagnosed with breast cancer. Greg McFall, God bless him, insisted on her having the best medical care. A radical mastectomy was performed at the Mayo Clinic, after which the prognosis was good, her doctors said.

Four

At Griffin, back then the local Catholic boys' college prep, I wallowed in mediocrity at first, struggling mightily with math, science, Latin, and intemperate behavior. Then, junior year, a couple of things happened: a Viatorian cleric-instructor unlocked for me the wonders of English literature and composition. Another priest, the school's prefect of discipline, gave me what would become a life-altering lecture: "With your looks, brains, and personality you are squandering your God-given talent and driving your poor mother nuts. Do you intend to be a jack-off forever?" the good padre inquired.

(Another Griffin High memory: in his dealings with a dozen or so gifted, cocky students, Rev. Arnold Perham, a physics teacher, would often tell us—obviously for motivational purposes—that once we got to college and beyond, "those big city kids would eat our lunch." I was part of that group despite mediocre academic achievement. It's now safe to say, fifty-plus years later with most of us retired, that we're still waiting for those big city kids to show up. In the meantime most of us became big city boys and quite successful ourselves.)

Eventually my grades improved enough to make the B honor roll, and I began writing—at first for the school newspaper and later as a stringer for my mom's former paper, the *Illinois State Register* (the *Journal-Register* today), covering mainly sports and police blotter incidents. My mother, whom I loved to please, was ecstatic about that, notwithstanding that her cancer had returned. She would have her other breast removed and undergo a vicious regimen of radiation treatments.

Back then as a teenager I pursued girls relentlessly but viewed dating and any related pleasurable accruals strictly as casual recreational perks—catch and release. Until, that is, the summer before my senior year at Griffin. I fell headlong in love when Kathleen Burke invited me to a Junior Women's Club dance. She was a cute, petite, bright, big-eyed junior-to-be at the all-girls Sacred Heart Academy who I'd seen around town and had coveted from a distance.

Our families knew and liked one another. Her grandfather, like mine, was a leading local figure in his profession. An 1898 graduate of the University of Michigan Law School, Edmund Burke's career started as an assistant state's attorney in the days when people in that line of work wore side arms. His early claim to fame was the successful prosecution of several members of the notorious Shelton Gang. They were to Downstate Illinois during their time what the Capone gang had been to Chicago. Later, in private practice, he served as personal attorney for Springfield resident John L. Lewis and represented the truculent labor leader's United Mine Workers.

Kathy and I were virtually inseparable early on, our bond cemented by less-than-idyllic home lives, especially hers. "You have splendid haunches," I'd tell her, "and you *will* be the mother of my children." My own mother's health continued to decline while my stepdad grew increasingly irascible; her parents withered in dead-end jobs and spent their spare time in alcoholic fogs, ignoring each other and their three children. Kathy and I found comfort and refuge in each other's company, not to mention each other's arms.

Greg McFall was a good man, but his mean streak was always lurking. Mostly he could be verbally abusive, and once or twice I thought I overheard him getting physically rough with my mother. She never said anything about it, nor did she show any visible signs of abuse, and denied it the one time I asked about it. (Looking back, ours was a small house, and they may simply have been having noisy sex.) However, once when I was sixteen and in full hormonal flower, I was showering, getting ready for a date. An excellent chef, Greg had been drinking much of the afternoon while barbecuing for a dinner party he and Mary Frances were hosting. He came in the house to use the facilities and asked in a rather acerbic tone how much longer I'd have our only bathroom tied up. My response was unnecessarily flippant and disrespectful, and he started throwing punches at me through the shower curtain. More startled than anything, I threw back the curtain and, stark naked, dripping wet, and covered with soapsuds, caught him with a right to the jaw. Down went McFall!

"If you ever touch me or my mother again I will kill you," I said calmly. It was a turning point in our relationship; it never happened again.

Five

As a teenager, I liked to take chances and hatch pranks. One of my personal favorites and biggest productions was a mock gangland-style killing. A friend, Mike Touch, owned a 1935 Hupmobile—a long, black, sinister-looking vehicle straight out of the Al Capone era. Late one summer evening several of us fellows were riding around town in the old car bored senseless, so I had an idea to break the monotony. We found a Laundromat on an out-of-the-way street. There was one person in the establishment at the time, a middle-aged woman. One of my buddies wearing a clean white shirt ran breathlessly into the place and began to use the pay phone.

"They're on to me! Jesus, you've got to get me out of this!" he cried into the receiver.

Just then, as planned, the Hupmobile pulled up in front of the place. The driver and I got out and entered. Wearing a fedora and sunglasses I took dead aim with a blank pistol and squeezed off three shots. The fellow on the phone clutched his chest and screamed as if in agony. The victim's shirt turned a brilliant red, and he sank to the floor. My sidekick and I collected our victim, dragged him out to the car, and sped off while the witness watched, horrified. We drove around the block and as we passed the coin laundry we saw that the woman was on the pay phone gesturing wildly—presumably trying to explain things to the authorities. The ersatz gangsters disposed of the shirt, soaked with chili sauce and ketchup, in a nearby trash bin and drove off to Don's, the local hamburger drive-in, to celebrate our cruel but apparently effective hoax.

Soon I graduated to more grown-up, rebellious escapades. Earlier I'd been asked to quit Boy Scouts for insubordination and in high school was banished from Key Club, a Kiwanis-sponsored youth service organization, when some others and I got drunk on cheap bourbon at the group's state convention in Peoria, stole some live lobsters from the hotel restaurant, and got caught by a chaperone as we were trying to race the stupid crustaceans down a corridor. I topped off the evening by throwing up. It was my first real experience with alcohol, and notwithstanding the awkward climax and a wicked hangover, I liked how it made me feel. It gave me courage and took the edge off of my insecurities, foreshadowing troubles to come.

Six

After high school it was on to follow in my mother's footsteps to study journalism at Marquette, the Jesuit university in Milwaukee. (In those days the emphasis was on objectivity, not the liberal bias and advocacy reporting that's so prevalent in the news media today, not to mention academia at-large.) I soon concluded that most of my fellow J-schoolers were largely homely, peculiar, unwashed, geeky, naïve misfits condemned to lives of occupational anonymity, financial drudgery, and personal bitterness working on newspapers or industrial trade publications. It also was evident after a couple of early writing courses designed to ferret out the terminally untalented that I could clear that critical hurdle handily, thanks largely to years of my mother's coaching and cajoling and a pencil-wielding editor back in Springfield at the *Journal-Register*. The attrition rate of my freshman J-school class was 50 percent.

(Besides my mother, her work, and an almost genetic attraction to the news media, my interest in journalism also was sparked by George Thiem, our Springfield neighbor and the state capital correspondent for the now-defunct *Chicago Daily News*. Thiem, whose son Teddy was a playmate, shared a Pulitzer Prize with Roy J. Harris of the *Post-Dispatch* in 1950 for exposing that several dozen newspaper reporters were also on the Illinois state payroll. Then, in 1956, Thiem won another Pulitzer, this time on his own, with the discovery that Orville Hodge, the Illinois auditor, embezzled of $2.5 million in state funds. Hodge subsequently was indicted, convicted, and served prison time. Thiem's work was spotlighted on *The Big Story*, an NBC network television program of the day that recognized investigative reporting achievements. Although it wasn't apparent at the time, I was also influenced by the 1962 critically acclaimed film *Days of Wine and Roses*, which traced the life and career of an alcoholic public relations executive and his wife.)

In March of my freshman year at Marquette, my mother lost her five-year battle with cancer. She was way too young, just forty-seven, and she'd been a profound influence while bestowing me with her passions for the English language and the mass media. Although her health had been declining for months, her death nevertheless tore a huge hole in my heart. But true to her example and my McCarthy heritage I shed no tears during the wake and funeral. Later, back home, I took a tranquilizer offered by a family doctor, washed it down with two beers, and cried myself to sleep. Mary Frances was more than a mom; she was a mentor, a life coach, and the only true parent I ever had. But I'd had eighteen years to practice the art of compartmentalization, and crushed as I was, I reckoned I'd have to do what she did after the loss of my father—suck it up, strap it on, and make my own way in life. No one else would or could do it for me. Besides, I'd already mastered the art of asphyxiating my emotions. And I was hell-bent to honor her memory, to make her proud.

Thankfully, Marquette and Milwaukee agreed with me. The midtown campus was within walking distance of three breweries and, outside the state's larger cities, the legal drinking age for beer was eighteen, so we took full advantage of it. Freshman year, two of my dorm wing mates were the sons of the CEOs of General Motors and Ford—James Roche Jr. and Paul (son of Semon "Bunky") Knudsen, respectively—giving me a rare and envious perspective on people of privilege—the fancy cars, the debutante gal pals, the sojourns to Aspen, Hawaii, or home to Grosse Pointe for the weekend, and the occasional debutante ball. One of my roommates, a spoiled rich kid from Chippewa Falls, owned an authentic automotive rarity—a bright red English-built 1959 Morgan roadster, which occasionally he'd let me borrow, and I'd use it to shuttle young ladies who were often queued up on Wisconsin Avenue hitchhiking from one end of campus to another.

Junior year, four other Marquette students and I lived together on the city's trendy East Side. Our apartment, at 1816 Kane Place just east of Prospect Avenue, overlooked Lake Michigan and the Milwaukee Yacht Club. It was party central.

Afternoons, November through March, we frequented varsity basketball practices, marveling at the antics of the school's brilliant, offbeat new head coach, legend-in-the-making Al McGuire. (In 1977, coaching his final game at Marquette, McGuire's Warriors won the NCAA championship, 67–59 over Dean Smith's North Carolina Tar Heels. McGuire went on to an enviable career as a college basketball analyst for CBS and NBC; he died in 2001 after a long battle with leukemia at the age of seventy-two.)

Another highlight: the Millard Fillmore Lecture delivered annually by a capped and gowned, alcohol-fueled philosophy professor, James "Pop" Murphy. With Professor Irwin Corey–like comic confusion, Murphy honored Fillmore on his birthday for having served with little distinction as our thirteenth president. Had it not been for old Millard, his twisted reasoning went, America would have no standard by which to judge its great presidents.

Back then traditional Greek social fraternities were banned at Marquette, so I threw in with the Chain Pullers, a rogue outfit that existed to play intramural sports, which we dominated, and to party. Our fight song was "The Ballad of Ira Hayes," Johnny Cash's ode to the tragic, flag-raising Native American hero of the Battle of Iwo Jima; we would break into it whenever several Chain Pullers got together and the spirit moved us, which was often:

"Call him drunken Ira Hayes
He don't answer any more
From the whiskey drinkin' Indian
To the Marine that went to war…"

At one point I decided the group needed a coat of arms to lend a little class and dignity to the organization. I set out to design a crest but abandoned the idea when it proved too cumbersome to portray, in Latin, the words "Intramural Invincibility, Perpetual Drunkenness, and Unlimited Gratification."

In early June 1966, I graduated with a bachelor's degree in journalism, a minor in economics, and a vague notion of what might be next.

A vocational epiphany of sorts occurred with back-to-back summer internships in the publicity department of the Illinois State Fair. I wrote news releases on coming attractions, staged special events to attract media attention, liaised with celebrity entertainers and their press agents, and had regular dealings with working reporters who appreciated punctual, accurate, and thorough responses to their questions and special requests. Once the fair opened in August I'd turn reporter myself, covering horse shows, livestock, cooking and other competitions, hustling back to the press center to post the results while alerting members of the regular reporter corps to any human interest feature story possibilities that may have surfaced on my rounds.

During the second summer on the job, with the fair in progress and my journalism degree in hand, I watched helpless and horrified along with several thousand other spectators as a catwalk jutting out over the grandstand crowd from its roof collapsed, causing several photographers to fall ninety feet to their deaths—the catwalk had been weakened by time and a taut rope used for twice-daily Green Beret rappelling demonstrations. It happened on August 20, a Saturday afternoon, just before the start of the annual one-hundred-mile USAC auto race. I was in the racetrack's infield at the time and saw it all. I commandeered a two-way radio from a security guard and called the office with early albeit sketchy details, which in turn were released to major news services via Teletype. The timeliness and accuracy of the release proved fortunate, as one of the wire services in the meantime had received and was moving an erroneous report that the entire grandstand roof collapsed with casualties numbering in the dozens, if not hundreds.

I did well enough at the state fair that the Illinois *State Journal* (now the *Journal-Register*) offered me a full-time reporting job paying a whopping $150 a week. By then, however, I felt my ultimate career destination would be somewhere other than newspaper work. I had a dream for myself all along, but it was still a bit fuzzy. Thanks to the state fair experience, I was beginning to get an idea what it might be—PR, public relations. Not only that, I was enthralled with the promise of the glitz, glamour, and gain that working for an agency might provide. I suppose it was a *Days of Wine and Roses* fantasy—with the accent metaphorically and decidedly more on the roses than the wine at that point. The wine, so to speak, would come later. But first there were dues to pay.

Seven

Kathy and I were on again, off again during college, but true to my word I proposed during the Thanksgiving break of my senior year. I graduated in June. We were married a month later and prepared to move to Saint Louis, one hundred miles south, where she had lined up a job teaching at an archdiocesan elementary school in suburban Kirkwood.

Living in Saint Louis was a lifelong dream. In the 1960s, the city had a powerful, almost transcendental allure—vibrancy, sophistication, glamour, wealth, culture, and a certain cosmopolitan yet old-world charm, clinging nevertheless desperately to its one-time grandeur (some sixty-five years earlier Saint Louis was the fourth largest city in America). A downtown riverfront renaissance was underway, sparked by the completion of the towering, majestic Gateway Arch, a new ballpark, and several impressive high-rise apartment and office buildings. Plus there was the paradoxically powerful gravitational pull of ancestry. I dreamed some day of raising my children in the city. Any sons, I hoped, would attend Saint Louis University High School, the superb Jesuit institution from which my father graduated in 1934. Established in 1818, it's the oldest secondary school west of the Mississippi River.

And then there were the Cardinals. For as long as I could remember I was a fan, and not just because they were the nearest Major League team. The franchise had a rich history, and there was no doubt I would have grown up in Saint Louis anyway had my dad returned from World War II. I saw my first ballgame at age five at the old Sportsman's Park and came to adore "Baseball's Perfect Warrior," the great Stan Musial.

During my youth I made dozens of pilgrimages to Saint Louis to stay with relatives, shop, attend sporting events, and, later on, to hook up with Kathy, who at that point was enrolled at Saint Louis University.

• • •

I was thirteen years old when on May 13, 1958, Musial got his three thousandth hit at Wrigley Field in Chicago. It was the final game of a road trip and a series with the Cubs, after which the Cardinals returned home via the Illinois Central Railroad. When the train pulled into Springfield there were several thousand people waiting to hail their conquering hero. A neighbor kid and I were in the crowd, having prevailed on my parents to drive us down to the IC depot. We were front and center when Stan, his wife, Lil, and the radio announcers, Joe Garagiola and Harry Caray, came to the platform. We got their autographs and then strolled down to the end of the train and hopped on. We found ourselves in the club car where other ballplayers were drinking, smoking, and playing cards. A conductor spotted us and threatened that unless we wanted to end up in Saint Louis we'd better get off the train. So depart we did, pronto.

Stan was ninety-two when he passed away early in 2013, ravaged by age and dementia. Before he died I would see him around town on a regular basis, and it was sad. One Saturday morning a year or so before he died he was having breakfast with his caretaker-grandson Brian Schwarze at Schneithorst's, a popular Saint Louis County restaurant. I went over, shook his hand, and recalled that idyllic day in May so many years before. When I mentioned he got his three thousandth hit that day off a Cubs pitcher named Moe Drabowski, another Polish American, he almost jumped out of his wheelchair and beaming exclaimed, "Moe Drabowski!" As we left the restaurant my wife noticed I was teary-eyed. "I can't help it," I said. "That's what happens when you see your boyhood hero—one of the great ballplayers of all time—diminished and in such a state." As the years went by Musial was all but forgotten despite his undeniable greatness and Hall of Fame status, overshadowed by the East Coast likes of Ted Williams, Joe DiMaggio, Mickey Mantle, and the more recent steroid-inflated feats of others. Thankfully, however, after all that time, he finally got a measure of the recognition he richly deserved, bestowed as he was in 2011 with the Presidential Medal of Freedom and as the subject of a fine biography by respected *New York Times* columnist George Vecsey.

• • •

Sadly, much of the allure and progressiveness Saint Louis once exhibited has all but vanished since the 1960s. The town lost its mojo. Two of the Big Three automakers have closed their assembly plants, a good portion of the Fortune 500 companies headquartered here have moved on or were swallowed up by bigger fish, local business and government leadership has been woefully lacking, and the community's reputation for racial division is hard to refute.

Eight

Once we were settled in Saint Louis, with Kathy teaching seventh and eighth grade math and science at a parochial grade school, I took a job with the public relations department of the Automobile Club (AAA), making sixty-five dollars a month *less* than my state fair summer job. In time I became responsible for turning out the club's monthly magazine and had various other duties. I worked for Ron Jacober, a good guy whose heart however was in broadcasting, and before long he embarked on a distinguished forty-year radio and TV career at KMOX Radio and KSDK-TV that earned him a well-deserved place in the Missouri Sports Hall of Fame.

The Auto Club was led back then by H. Sam Priest, a former high-profile head of the Board of Police Commissioners, who fancied himself as an intellectual, running with a circle of Washington University intelligentsia. He spoke in a falsetto voice, washed his hands incessantly, and was obsessed with the idea of computerizing the Auto Club's operations—emergency road service as well as the administrative functions. Shortly after starting work there I wrote a rather provocative 750-word analysis of local gasoline pricing for our three-hundred-thousand-circulation magazine; the piece was reprinted in "The Mirror of Public Opinion," then the op-ed page of the *Post-Dispatch*—heady stuff for a twenty-two-year-old rookie.

One of Mr. Priest's cronies was a former newspaper man and Ford Foundation staffer, Martin Quigley, who worked at a PR firm called Fleishman-Hillard and to whom Sam paid a monthly retainer just to show up occasionally—often with a black eye or facial bruises, trophies of his perpetual carousing. He would spend an hour or so with Priest and then pop down to our office to make ridiculous suggestions that he'd already vetted with the boss. But as a result I became even more intrigued with the notion of consulting—working for an agency with clients, challenges, and a chance to make some real money.

(Quigley attained some modest celebrity as the ghostwriter for Joe Garagiola's *Baseball Is a Funny Game,* a behind-the-scenes look at the humorous things that went on between the foul lines and in the clubhouses of our national pastime. It was the best-selling baseball book ever for ten years until Jim Bouton wrote *Ball Four,* a memoir, published in 1970.)

After a year and a half with AAA, I was lured to the staff of the fledgling Saint Louis campus of the University of Missouri (UMSL). My boss, Robert E. "Bob" Smith, was a former political reporter who made the move to city hall as press secretary to Mayor Ray Tucker and then on to the McDonnell Douglas Aviation Company (now Boeing), where the eccentric founder, J. S. McDonnell, still ran the show with a tight, stingy fist during the early swashbuckling Mercury, Gemini, and Apollo eras of America's space program. Before all of that, as a young University of Missouri J-School grad, Bob Smith chronicled the heroic and sometimes bizarre World War II escapades of General George S. Patton for *Stars and Stripes,* the military newspaper. There he ran with another cub reporter who later would achieve fame and followers as an ageless, irrepressible media curmudgeon—the late Andy Rooney. Smith knew everything and everybody in town and was a perfect mentor.

No sooner did I begin working for the university than came shocking notice that my "sole surviving son" deferment had been revoked, making me eligible for the military draft. I was determined to fight the reclassification, insisting that once the sole surviving son of a parent killed in combat, always a sole surviving son. The government maintained, however, that since my mother was no longer living, my deferment was of no comfort to a surviving spouse. The problem was that my mother had been dead for three years when I was granted the deferment in the first place.

(Little wonder why I have a jaundiced view of government and have come to believe that there is always a solution, even to the most thorny problems, if you're willing to take risks and fight like hell. So I did.)

General Lewis Hershey headed the Selective Service System in those days. At age seventy-five Hershey was the oldest four-star general in history and the only one to attain that rank without ever having seen combat action. He had a J. Edgar Hoover–like hold on the draft system and literally answered to no one. I was motivated by that and by the fact that I had a wife and we'd begun our careers, to say nothing of the lack of fairness. Induction almost certainly would mean a tour of duty in Vietnam.

My appeals were unsuccessful, however, and I'd received orders to report for basic training when I learned of a similar case—another fellow in the same predicament had refused induction and was convicted of draft evasion. The US Supreme Court agreed to hear his case (McKart vs. US), putting my departure on hold until the high court ruled. They did so, finally finding for the defendant by a vote of nine to nothing! I was off the hook; had it not been for dogged determination, a sense of justice, and some blind luck, I most likely would have ended up toting an M-16 in a rice paddy somewhere in Southeast Asia.

In the three years following our marriage, both of Kathy's parents died of cancer before reaching the age of fifty, and stepdad Greg McFall Sr. succumbed suddenly, the victim of an abdominal aneurysm, at sixty-two. That left us with no living parents or stepparents, depriving the children we ultimately would have of grandparents. Despite our clashes over the years, I'd grown close to my stepdad and felt his loss deeply. However, I was not so moved by the demise of my in-laws, which put a decided damper on the succor I was able to provide my young bride. My penchant for compartmentalization and burying emotions kicked in big time.

I spent nearly four years as a Bob Smith understudy, devouring his wisdom while helping to establish the newest University of Missouri campus as a legitimate player on the higher education scene. With the Vietnam conflict raging, the Kent State massacre, the Martin Luther King Jr. and

Bobby Kennedy assassinations, and an America getting high and dropping out with drugs, sex, and rock 'n' roll, it was an exhilarating time to be on a college campus. Despite my usual focus and intensity, I was not immune from the many temptations at hand. It was a veritable smorgasbord of spirits, weed, and horny students, faculty, and faculty wives. I smoked pot on several occasions, but did not like its energy-sapping effect. The same was not true of Scotch, rum, and beer, which helped make me smarter, wittier, better looking, and an all-around greater guy, or so it seemed at the time.

Before long we had our first child, a son we named Matthew, and I felt added pressure to move along with my career. I put out a few feelers and before long was back in Springfield interviewing for a job with the administration of Governor Richard Ogilvie, a Republican and the former sheriff of Cook County, who soon would be up for reelection. I was assigned to a new bureaucracy—the state's Environmental Protection Agency. The mission: to help establish the agency, gaining public acceptance for the recently enacted laws it enforced while testing the viability of its director, a peculiar former state legislator from the Chicago suburbs, for selection as Ogilvie's second term running mate. The best thing about it: I'd be making 40 percent more money.

After having spent five years in Saint Louis, I found Springfield suffocating. I burned the candle at both ends, crisscrossing the state by car and small planes and hanging out in all the "official" state capital watering holes, neglecting husbandly duties whenever I was home. The agency's interests were being well enough served, but it was doubtful that Ogilvie would be elected to a second term, and it was virtually certain that my immediate boss, the EPA director, would not make the ticket anyway. Besides, I was a fish out of water; I didn't have the requisite political pedigree—no YGOP credentials or campaign experience—a deficiency I was not-so-subtly reminded of regularly by coworkers and others. So while I felt a bit out of place in terms of political chops, at least the compelling, common sense wisdom of conservatism and the merits of a free-market economy were beginning to come into focus for me.

Then an Air Illinois commuter plane carrying six young EPA staff lawyers—all of whom I'd worked with and respected—went down in a violent thunderstorm near Peoria en route from Chicago's Meigs Field to Springfield, killing all onboard. I'd taken that flight four or five times a month during the relatively short time I'd been on the job. I saw it as an omen.

(For the uninitiated, I try to explain that the practice of public relations typically involves the use of various communications strategies and tactics to help organizations foster a positive reputation, to create buzz about or to help sell products or services, to deal with crisis situations, to articulate positions on issues, and the like. Without exception the written word, content, is central to both traditional journalism and public relations, which explains our early focus on hiring newspaper people and other experienced reporters. In PR, virtually everything depends fundamentally on solid writing—content is king and remains so to this day. It also entails significant counselling and interpretation of how an organization's actions, or failure to act will impact the media, stakeholder groups and/or the public at large. PR is not the same as advertising and should not be confused with it, although with the advent of social media and mergers of PR and ad agencies, those distinctions have blurred somewhat.)

Nine

Barely six months into the Illinois job, salvation came with a call out of the blue from my old UM-Saint Louis boss, Bob Smith. "I know you've only been up there a short time, and you're probably not anxious to move again so soon, but there's an opening at Fleishman-Hillard, and I've recommended you to my friend Harry Wilson, their chairman," he said.

I did not know Wilson personally, only by reputation, as a consummate, hard-boiled professional. But I did know Fleishman-Hillard, having become familiar with the agency during my first stint in Saint Louis. They had a sterling reputation as the agency of record for many of the city's top companies and a host of other organizations—a blue chip client roster led by brewing behemoth Anheuser-Busch. Moreover, the idea of working in an agency appealed to a simmering, as-yet-untapped entrepreneurial urge.

Kathy exploded when I told her about a possible return to Saint Louis. We'd just learned she was pregnant again, and she insisted she could not deal with another move so soon. Besides, she liked being back in her hometown. "I appreciate that, but this gig is headed nowhere, and we have to be ready when a big opportunity presents itself. This could be it," I insisted.

So the following Saturday morning, on the sly, I made the ninety-minute drive to Saint Louis for a first interview with Harry Wilson and Fleishman-Hillard.

Alfred Fleishman and Robert Hillard may have been the namesake founders and original prime movers of the agency, but Harry Wilson was its cerebral and cultural cortex. A former reporter whose career began with United Press International in Kansas City where he shared a desk with a young Walter Cronkite, Wilson was a workaholic who frequently got to the office at 3:00 or 4:00 a.m., behavior partially due to narcolepsy, a chronic condition that could cause him to fall asleep anytime, anywhere. He controlled it with Dexedrine, sometimes not all that well. As I would learn soon enough, on big snow days Wilson would circulate a staff memo saluting those who had made it in to work on time. We called it "The Honor Roll of the Intrepid" and it served, coincidentally, to reinforce the firm's herculean work ethic. In those days before computers it took two secretaries to process the prodigious volume of work Wilson turned out, and he had another typist on call around the clock to deal with any overflow the others couldn't handle. Flinty and rather self-conscious, he was tall, lanky, crusty, and utterly unpretentious, as exemplified by the fingernails he chewed when nervous, the crew cut he wore all his life, and the Ford Pinto he drove for a good portion of it. I liked him instantly. (Several years before I joined the firm, Fleishman and Hillard decided to expand the agency's ownership. They bestowed partnerships to Harry Wilson and another fellow and added their names formally to that of the organization. However, things didn't work out with one of the two new partners and he exited the agency, prompting the humble surviving Wilson, classically, to insist on a return to the Fleishman-Hillard marquee rather than one that retained his name.)

The interview with Wilson went well, and the following weekend I was invited to return to Saint Louis and the firm's riverfront office to meet with John Graham, a rising young star within the agency who, word had it, was being groomed for bigger things. I found Graham charming, bright, and, most importantly, interested. Disarmingly slight of stature and build and studious in demeanor, the effect magnified back then by oversized horn-rimmed glasses, he attended the University of Missouri on a dual athletic and academic scholarship and was a mainstay sprinter on the track team before graduating with a journalism degree. We clicked, and he offered me the job for $288 a year *less* than I was making with the State of Illinois. To me it was all about the promise of life in the private sector and a shot at being entrepreneurial. (Instinctively I believed that in the long run if I did well at the job, income, status, responsibility, and the rest would take care of themselves. And privately I vowed that I would never lobby for pay or position; hopefully I wouldn't have to.)

Ten

Nineteen seventy-two was an eventful year. President Richard Nixon made a historic visit to Chairman Mao and China. Over Vietnam, the United States bombed Haiphong and Hanoi. The Watergate break-in happened in June, while the crew of Apollo 16 spent a record seventy-one hours on the Moon. Don McLean's "American Pie" was the top song on the hit parade. PLO terrorists scorched the Munich Olympics, killing eleven Israelis. The Oakland As won the World Series, besting the Cincinnati Reds. The Miami Dolphins would not lose a single NFL game all season. The first of the twin towers of New York's imposing, since-lamented World Trade Center opened for business. And, while history took no note of it, on February 1 at the age of twenty-seven, I reported for duty at Fleishman-Hillard, Inc. I was going to be an agency man, believed it was my calling, and I could barely contain myself.

I arrived at the agency all bright-eyed and bushy-headed, a white boy sporting the closest thing possible to an Afro, notwithstanding a fast-receding hairline, if not because of it.

My new firm had several dozen primo clients, lavish new office space—the entire 9,500-square-foot sixth floor of One Memorial Drive, the sparkling CBS Gateway Tower building at the south leg of the Gateway Arch—a staff of two-dozen people, and billings of just under $1 million. The building crackled with activity and excitement—bursting with an abundance of glitz, talent, hormones, and possibility. The CBS-owned KMOX radio and television stations occupied floors one through four. D'Arcy, the advertising agency for Anheuser-Busch and other blue chip clients, had a block of floors upstairs. Ditto one of the (then) Big Eight accounting firms. The top floor housed the executive offices of Union Electric, the regional utility, also an F-H client.

I still hadn't met Alfred Fleishman or Bob Hillard when I reported for work. A pharmacist by formal training, Fleishman's first love was local politics. Hillard, a Phi Beta Kappa University of Minnesota grad, was a reporter for the defunct *Saint Louis Star-Times.* They met and became friendly in the early 1940s when Fleishman was serving as deputy clerk of the circuit courts and Hillard covered the municipal beat—the courts and city hall. Returning to Saint Louis after World War II they decided there was a better way to make a living than they had antebellum, and in 1946 they started their agency in five hundred square feet of space above a Woolworth's five and dime store at Grand and Olive Streets in Midtown Saint Louis. It was the two of them plus Margaret Jackson, serving as an office manager and secretary, and who later would become Mrs. Bob Hillard.

Early on, Fleishman was the front man for the firm. Savvy and gregarious, he had excellent connections around town and was responsible for attracting clients. Hillard, on the other hand, was less flamboyant yet no wallflower and a superb thinker and writer; he turned out most of the work product. Together they were a formidable duo, and in short order they had a stable of eight or nine clients and decided they needed to hire another communicator to keep pace with their growth. Enter Harry Wilson.

That first day as I was unpacking and getting familiar with my new surroundings, a partial eclipse occurred; an imposing human figure appeared in my office doorway, casting a massive shadow over my desk.

"You must be Finnigan," he boomed. "I'm Bob Hillard. Welcome aboard. I hope they're taking good care of you. You available for lunch?"

"You bet I am, Mr. Hillard, and thanks, I'm delighted to be here. I've heard a lot about you; it's great to finally meet you."

"Call me Bob, please. I'll drop by around lunchtime. We'll head over to the Stadium Club, if that's OK." Hillard was a tall, heavy-set figure in his late fifties who spoke in a resonant bass that blared through the office as if amplified electronically. He was bald, bearded, and bespectacled—a man of relatively few words, all well-chosen. "Don't let the bellowing fool you. Mr. Hillard is a pussycat," my new secretary said once he'd moved on, "and he's like a father to most of us."

The next visitor was Ruth Jacobson, the grand dame of Saint Louis special events. She struck me as brusque, shrill, dismissive, self-important, scatterbrained, and vectoring quickly toward the menopausal cusp. After twenty years with Fleishman-Hillard she knew just about everyone on the town's social register and how to play them, and no one would think of attempting a grand opening, a groundbreaking, or a charity benefit event without enlisting her involvement. "I understand you'll be helping out with the Marriott Hotel opening," she said with just a hint of condescension. "Let's get together this afternoon, and I'll bring you up to speed."

"Great, I'm looking forward to it," I replied.

At lunch I found Bob Hillard down-to-earth, brimming with wisdom, and with many interesting, amusing, and relevant tales to tell. Clearly he cared deeply about the firm and its people. As a die-hard Cardinals fan, I also found the elegant private club that looked out on the ball field to be a real treat. "I could get used to this," I thought to myself, dazzled by the setting, the service, the food, and most of all the civic big shots and sports luminaries who lunched on all sides of us.

As for client responsibilities, Hillard said I'd be working on Granite City Steel, Union Electric (now Ameren), and The 7UP Company in addition to helping Mrs. Jacobson with her hotel event. "You'll do well here," Hillard predicted as we were about to part company back at the office. Then he did something I found rather unusual but refreshing: he thanked me for having lunch with him, even though he'd been the host. Classy.

Margaret Hillard died of cancer a short time later. Ironically, neither Bob nor Al Fleishman had children of their own—heirs to pass their interests along to or to bring into the business. As they viewed the world, the firm was their family, and their children, so to speak, were John Graham plus eventually me and other next-generation men and women on whose brains and backs the agency would travel where destiny, skill, and hard work would take it. Al Fleishman and Bob Hillard had the original vision and took the risks required to launch an extraordinary agency with solid values and unlimited potential. It was up to us to take it from there.

• • •

Upon arriving for Ruth Jacobson's meeting to discuss the hotel opening, I was handed a packet containing a rundown of the planned event and drafts of news releases and other documents she'd prepared for the extravaganza. "We have to make a huge, spectacular splash," the diva declared. "Both Marriotts—Bill Senior and Junior—will be here. We're using an aviation theme since the hotel is at the airport and Saint Louis has a rich flight heritage. An exact replica of Lindbergh's Spirit of Saint Louis will be on display outside the hotel. (It was in fact the very Ryan NX 211 monoplane used in the eponymous 1957 biopic, starring James Stewart as Charles Lindbergh, and which today is on display at the Missouri History Museum.) We'd hoped to have a small plane cut the ribbon, but the FAA won't allow it because it's too dangerous—too close to Lambert Field and the space is too tight for a plane to fly through."

I reviewed the materials and was a bit surprised at how shabbily written they were. These will never do, I thought, so I fine-tuned the copy and then made an inquiry: "I can understand why they'd balk at a fixed wing aircraft, but what about a helicopter?" Jacobson's eyes lit up. "Is that possible?" I contacted a local chopper service and the next day we met with them at the hotel to assess the situation. The pilot, a former Vietnam gunship driver with nerves of steel, said he could break a ribbon suspended from the top of the hotel building stretched across to an adjacent flagpole, provided it was made of a lightweight cloth that would break on contact and not get tangled in his rotor blades. There was ample clearance between the building and the flagpole, he said. And there'd be a bonus, he predicted: "When I come roaring around the corner of the building, blast through the target space, and nip that ribbon, it'll startle the crap out of the spectators and be a great visual to boot." That was a very good thing, I reasoned, so long as his flying machine remained airborne.

In a couple of days the FAA approved the use of the helicopter, and I found a source for a flimsy but functional foot-deep red ribbon that could be stretched from the top of the hotel building across to the intended flagpole, approximately one hundred feet in the air and about the same distance across.

The big day arrived. With both Marriotts—father and son—and a host of local dignitaries watching from the hotel's top-floor restaurant, the helicopter blasted flawlessly through the narrow space on cue and clipped the ribbon with its runners as thousands of helium-filled balloons were released and a high school band played "Wild Blue Yonder." It left the VIPs breathless. Local TV crews captured the stunt for the evening news and fed their footage nationally. The stage was set for a gala black tie dinner dance that evening benefiting the Missouri Historical Society and featuring Woody Herman's Orchestra. Practically every local luminary attended.

Basking in the glow of her latest success, Madame Jacobson told me privately that I'd done a good job. There was no mention of the rewrite I did on her handout materials or the helicopter coup. Baptism.

• • •

I think it was Graham who, as I joined the firm, said he'd be curious to see how I stacked up against another fair-haired boy who'd gone to work at F-H not long before I got there, a former college classmate of his. If he was trying to see what I was made of it worked. I was eager to take this other fellow's measure, and in short order it was clear to me that if I couldn't outperform him I didn't belong in the agency business. Within a couple of years he'd pretty much gone as far as he could and decided to change careers. Me? I was embarking on a dream come true, bolstered by a growing awareness that I felt very much at home in the agency game.

Eleven

So I continued to cut my agency teeth, helping Granite City Steel capitalize on a major pollution control initiative in response to an enforcement action by my old Illinois state agency, the IEPA. For Union Electric, the regional utility, I handled the supersensitive disclosure of plans to build a nuclear power plant in rural Calloway County in mid-Missouri. And for 7UP, then still a Saint Louis-based independent soft drink company basking in the glow of the breakthrough Uncola ad campaign, I wrote and produced my first ever annual report to shareholders and drafted speeches for the CEO and other senior executives use at an international sales convention in Mexico City. Things were going swimmingly, but it didn't take long for me to feel a bit bored and underutilized.

(It was the early 70s and a technological revolution was on the immediate horizon, altering forever how business and communications would be conducted. In those days, however, we were still using typewriters; widespread use of word processing computers was still a few years away; primitive document transmission devices known as telecopiers had yet to be replaced by fax machines and other technology; television newsrooms were just beginning to use videotape in place of film for their on-location reports, and satellite feeds were still a decade away. The Internet—social media, blogs, viral marketing, and the like? Not for another twenty years or more.)

As I ploughed through assignments at the office, Kathy gave birth to our second child, a son we named Brendan. In some respects, as an emotional cripple of sorts, home life and fatherhood were more challenging and mysterious for me than the public relations business. Perhaps that was due to my own upbringing. I was proud of my sons and deeply in love with them and tried when I could to help with the unending demands of a newborn and a precocious two-year-old, but somehow I was not always able to exhibit the joy and warmth I felt for them and my work, ever intoxicating, kept me away from home a great deal. I look back on those days with guilt and regret.

Early on I worked with Hillard, Wilson, and Graham but had little contact with Al Fleishman, a.k.a. Moses. He was preoccupied—immersed in his own assignments and other interests, functioning almost as a separate agency within the firm, what with the never-ending demands of Anheuser-Busch, his writing and lecturing on public relations and general semantics, plus fund-raising and advocacy work for various Jewish causes, including the State of Israel, which he visited frequently.

Fleishman also helped Joe Garagiola get his start in broadcasting. A retired journeyman Major League catcher who grew up with Yogi Berra on The Hill, Saint Louis's working class Italian sector, the gregarious Garagiola needed help early on with both elocution and diction. Fleishman drilled and grilled him without mercy until he was airworthy. (Another original F-H staffer, the erstwhile Martin Quigley, ghostwrote Garagiola's book *Baseball Is a Funny Game,* which for a couple of decades was the best-selling baseball book of all time. Quig, as he was known, was long gone by the time I arrived at F-H, presumably done in by his prodigal lifestyle.) In 1955 after cutting his broadcasting teeth with Harry Caray and Jack Buck on Cardinals radio broadcasts, Joe moved on and up to work network television baseball games and to cohost NBC's *Today* show and various game shows. (In 1991, Garagiola was enshrined in the broadcasters wing of the Baseball Hall of Fame.)

To me, on the one hand Fleishman was brilliant and gutsy. On the other, he could be condescending, brash, and exceptionally indiscreet given the nature of our business. He was somewhat a Renaissance man—an accomplished photographer, a passable musician, and a reputed expert on general semantics, the impact of one's words on others, having authored several books on the topic. Yet he thought nothing of calling someone a fool or an idiot to his or her face, impugning his personal credibility, to say nothing of the effect it could have on his targeted victim. Complicating factors, Fleishman was not well regarded by young, hard-charging August Busch III, who he treated without proper deference given his birthright and the inevitability that someday soon he would assume the helm of the brewery, which at that point was still led by his flamboyant, aging father, August A. "Gussie" Busch Jr. (Eventually, as Busch III ascended to power, John Graham masterfully persuaded him to retain Fleishman-Hillard as his company's agency of record so that we could show what we could do, promising a new cast of professionals who'd be dedicated to the brewery account.)

Fleishman's office door was adorned with a large-format black and white photo of himself taken by the celebrated photographer Herb Weitman. It depicted Alfred chewing his fingernails and was captioned, "There will always be a PR man." After a year or so with the firm, photographer Jim Clarke took a candid photo of me atop the coke ovens at Granite City Steel. I was wearing a hard hat, sunglasses under safety goggles and, over my nose, a triangular mask fitted with a filter to minimize breathing the oven's toxic fumes. I looked otherworldly. Clarke gave me a large print of the shot, which I had mounted on foam board. I hung it on my office wall with a caption that read, "There will always be a PR thing."

Fleishman devoted his agency time almost exclusively to Mr. Busch Jr. In the early 1950s he helped convince the elder Busch to buy the Saint Louis Cardinals for $3.7 million, saving the ball club for Saint Louis. Contrary to common impression, Busch was never a particularly avid baseball fan, but he relished the halo of civic adoration that came from the ownership, and the team's value as a promotional vehicle for his company's products was not lost in the equation. Alfred did not miss a trick with Gussie and the baseball franchise: he had the old man don a Cardinals jersey and visit with the players during preseason workouts—delighting the news media on hand. Several years later, Al urged the beer baron to caution the city fathers of Saint Petersburg, Florida, that the team would abandon its spring training facilities there if the growing number of African American players on the club was not permitted to stay in the same hotels and dine at the same restaurants as their white counterparts. It was a public relations masterstroke, not to mention the right thing to do.

Against Fleishman's advice, however, Gussie tried to change the name of old Sportsman's Park where the Cardinals played their home games to Budweiser Stadium. Baseball Commissioner Ford Frick nixed the move anyway, saying it was tasteless and blatantly too commercial, so the canny Gussie went with his second choice—Busch Stadium. Shortly thereafter he introduced a popular priced beer known as Busch Bavarian. (Today, of course, many if not most pro sport venues have commercial names, the rights fees for which generate many millions of dollars for teams and/or their local stadium authorities.)

Always in command, Busch Jr. bristled when a young pitcher, Steve Carlton, showed up with facial hair and demanded a $5,000 raise to continue to play for the Cardinals. "Get rid of him," Gussie ordered general manager Bing Devine, and Carlton was traded to the Philadelphia Phillies. The big left-hander went on to win 329 games during his career, and in 1994 was enshrined in baseball's Hall of Fame in Cooperstown, New York.

Nevertheless, the Cardinals won three National League pennants and two world championships in the 1960s, including a miraculous, seminal victory over the mighty New York Yankees in the 1964 World Series. They added three more pennants and a World Series in the 1980s, all during the ownership of Anheuser-Busch.

Twelve

My dream all along—even before day one at F-H—was to work on the Anheuser-Busch business, and I'd made no secret of it to the powers that be. As it happened, I didn't have to wait too long for my first encounter with the brewery and old Gussie Busch, and baseball was the connection. After an eleven-day players strike in 1972, "The Big Eagle," as Busch Jr. was known, was disgusted and spoke privately and often about selling the Cardinals. Richard A. Meyer, at the time a brewery vice president who also served as president of the ball club, called Al Fleishman and said, "We have to stop him." They decided that perhaps if the old man was reminded how well known and admired he was as a result of the Cardinals ownership and how closely sports fans identified with his beer brands, he'd change his mind. They contracted with Chilton Opinion Research of Philadelphia to do two surveys—one of sports fans and beer drinkers inside Cardinals country, and one covering the rest of the United States. At Graham's suggestion Fleishman asked me to help, coordinating the project and serving as go-between with Chilton in developing the questions and later on in presenting the findings to Mr. Busch. The scheme worked. With a lump in my throat and in a voice perhaps half an octave higher than usual I presented the summarized findings to the old man. The survey showed exactly what they suspected and hoped it would. Busch Jr. was impressed and appeased. The team remained in the hands of Anheuser-Busch for another twenty-five years; to this day Cardinals fans don't know how close the brewery was to selling the franchise in the early 1970s. As barely more than an agency rookie, it didn't occur to me until later that if the survey results had been otherwise, or if Busch Jr. did not like the cut of my jib, it might have been me rather than the clever Fleishman who'd take the hit.

Nevertheless, I relished the opportunity to interact with the visionary, colorful, and legendary brewing magnate and civic benefactor—the gravel-voiced titan who adorned the cover of *Time* magazine in July 1955 and *Sports Illustrated* in May 1957, who had introduced the magnificent Clydesdale horses to the world as Prohibition ended in 1933, and was credited with many other industry innovations and promotional firsts.

(For decades Fleishman-Hillard handled all external communications for Anheuser-Busch, advertising excluded of course. The brewery had no in-house PR department in those days, leaving F-H responsible for media relations, special events, financial and crisis communications, and various other duties.)

Thirteen

Bob Hillard's wife, Margaret, died of cancer shortly after I joined the firm, leaving him alone in the world and emotionally pulverized. He was drinking heavily. On one occasion when he failed to show up at the office or to answer his phone, Harry Wilson and John Graham found him sprawled on the floor of his showcase South Saint Louis bungalow on the bluffs overlooking the Mississippi River. Before long, however, both he and Al Fleishman announced their intentions to retire. Hillard quit drinking and later met and married Dr. Nancy Oxenhandler, a respected practicing clinical psychologist and author. They left town and spent their remaining years together in a remote rustic hideaway near Caledonia in the Ozarks, one hundred miles southwest of the city, reachable only after a half-mile trek from the main road down a dirt path and fording a creek. Hillard then turned to raising chickens, bees, and, for the rest of his life, very little hell.

(In March of 2000, with Hillard on the brink of death, the late *Post-Dispatch* feature writer John Michael McGuire was assigned to write a story for the paper on Hillard's life and career, so he and I and talented F-H colleague Paul Wagman, a former *Post-Dispatch* reporter, drove down to Caledonia to interview Bob. Although he clearly knew he did not have long to live, Hillard was alert, energetic, and most accommodating—in a sense geared up for what he sensed would be his final performance. When we finished, sensing I'd probably never see him again, I gave him a kiss on the top of his bald head, thanked him, and told him I loved him. He died that night. McGuire's story appeared in the paper a day or two later. It was a fitting send-off for a wonderful man and a true honor to have spent some of his final hours with him. Bob Hillard was eighty-two.)

Alfred Fleishman died in 2002, just shy of his ninety-seventh birthday.

Fourteen

One day a couple of years after I joined F-H, a young woman appeared in the office. She'd been hired as an assistant to the mercurial diva Ruth Jacobson. She was twenty-three and one of the most fetching creatures I'd ever laid eyes on. She was statuesque with a great figure, high cheekbones, and dazzling blue eyes that did her Lithuanian-German lineage proud. Her name was Connie Simokaitis and, as I would come to learn, she was whip smart, deeply caring, and, ironically, grew up in South Saint Louis four or five blocks from where my father was raised. I couldn't help myself.

"Roses are red. Violets are blue. What color are yours?" I inquired.

"Wouldn't you like to find out?" she responded gamely.

"You bet," I volleyed, and invited her to have a drink with me "so as to delve further into that and other cosmic uncertainties."

Obviously she could flirt; I was determined to see if there was more where that came from.

• • •

At about the same time, I was banging away on my trusty big gray Royal manual typewriter one day, my back turned to the office door, when a diminutive visitor interrupted my concentration. Actually, I heard him before I saw him; the voice was unmistakable.

"That cheap-ass SOB," he said, obviously in a state of high dudgeon.

"Who's a cheap-ass SOB?" I asked.

"Hyland," came the response, the complaint issued by a twenty-three-year-old Bob Costas, who'd been brought to town fresh out of Syracuse University to be the radio voice of the erstwhile Spirits of Saint Louis of the old American Basketball Association (ABA). The Hyland in question was the man who'd done the bringing—the legendary Robert Hyland, CBS vice president and the general manager of mighty KMOX. (In those days KMOX was owned and operated by CBS.)

"Do you have any idea what he's paying me?" Costas asked, he having traveled by elevator all the way up to our sixth floor office from the station's studios, three floors below, just to rant and rave. (I'd befriended him shortly after his arrival in Saint Louis. We were both big admirers of Coach Al McGuire and writer Pete Axthelm.)

"I'd guess about nineteen thousand dollars a year," I ventured.

"To the penny," he replied, a bit incredulous over the accuracy of my guesstimate.

"Don't you think I'm worth more than that? After all, in addition to the ballgames he has me doing morning drop-ins to serve as Jack Carney's stooge, plus hosting sports talk and occasional late night programming! I'm meeting myself coming and going and what do I have to show for it?"

"Look," I said, "you're working for one of the most powerful men in broadcasting. He's a giant in his profession, a genius and a star-maker. He hired you, didn't he? You're learning your craft, paying your dues. Obviously if Hyland didn't think you have what it takes you wouldn't have these opportunities, or that exposure. Look at all the talent he's helped develop—Jack Buck, Harry Caray, Joe Garagiola, Dan Kelly, Mike Shannon, Dan Dierdorf—the list goes on and on. You have enormous talent and the potential to become a big name in your own right; the sky's the limit as to how far you can go. Now hop back on that elevator and get back to work." Hop he did, and in relatively short order went on to have a brilliant career broadcasting sports at the network level.

Fifteen

Dennis Patrick Long was a rising star at Anheuser-Busch, working as the executive assistant to August Busch III, heir-apparent to the helm of the brewing empire and even then, in his early thirties, fast emerging as a key company executive.

One day Long called a meeting of agency types to discuss "Pitch In!," a new antilitter ad campaign a brewing industry association group was getting set to launch, underwritten by Anheuser-Busch and produced by the D'Arcy agency. John Graham tapped me to accompany him to the meeting, presumably because I had environmental experience and had fared well with my early assignments, including coordination of the super hush-hush Chilton baseball ownership survey. The unwritten part was that Long saw it as an opportunity to instill some new blood and thinking into the brewery's programs, thus the presence of Graham and Finnigan rather than Al Fleishman for whom Busch III had little use, and Al's team, which consisted of a couple of shopworn assistants. Long's objective was to get as much PR mileage out of the campaign as possible, a demonstration of his well-honed instincts.

As the meeting progressed he asked what those present thought of the campaign, ultimately coming around to me. "I like the jingle. It's got a good beat, and I'll bet it's easy to dance to. On a scale of one to ten I'd give it a seven point five," my American Bandstand-inspired volubility neither wasted on nor appreciated by the ad agency folks in the room. While Long and the others stewed, I turned serious: "This is a stop-gap measure. It's OK as far as it goes, but at best it will only buy some time and maybe some goodwill from those pressuring the industry to make real changes. In the meantime, the company and its suppliers need to find new ways to package beer and collect and reuse packaging materials. Let's hope that's happening because this campaign will have a brief lifespan. And there's no guarantee it won't draw fire from environmentalists—for superficiality. We need to be ready for that too." At first, Graham appeared to cringe; he wasn't sure what to think of my glibness or the candor, but Long was impressed. The campaign kickoff went as planned. The results were as predicted. Denny Long wanted more of my time. Recognizing the possibilities for our agency, Graham was only too happy to oblige, and while it wouldn't be apparent until later, my pull-no-punches approach would become a personal trademark—usually, but not always, for the better. And of course I was on cloud nine.

Soon Long was named to head the company's non-beer business units—amusement parks, real estate development, and a bakery products unit that decades earlier helped the company weather Prohibition and the Great Depression. He'd started with Anheuser-Busch fresh out of high school as an elevator operator and office boy. A product of a working-class Irish Catholic family, he caught the eye of Busch III in the 1960s, and after several interim assignments became the scion's executive assistant. He was bright, resourceful, hard-working, diplomatic, and well organized. And we clicked instantly.

For his theme park marketing chief Long chose W. Munro "Monty" Roberts III, a brilliant, occasionally berserk product of an aristocratic Saint Louis family. Roberts was a Yale dropout with a doctorate in prodigality earned largely on the sidewalks and in the bistros of Gaslight Square, Saint Louis's latter-day adult entertainment zone and a launching pad for the careers of performers like Barbra Streisand, Woody Allen, Stiller & Meara, the Smothers Brothers, and others. He was tall and movie-star-handsome with a booming voice, curly gray hair, and blue eyes, which earned him the tag of "Paul Newman's Grandfather." He'd previously worked in the advertising business in New York and then for Lee Iacocca at Ford, managing the company's motor sports and helping to introduce the Cougar, Mercury's version of the enormously successful Mustang. As such, he had a hefty roster of legitimate contacts in advertising, public relations, mass media, and auto racing.

At Long's urging, Roberts called to introduce himself. "What do you know about theme parks?" Roberts asked. "Nothing. Why?" I responded. But I had a hunch why he was asking. He explained the company owned 3,600 acres of land east of historic Williamsburg, Virginia, on which it had built a brewery and was under construction with Kingsmill, a fashionable residential and resort community on the venerable James River, and a $40 million European-themed Busch Gardens family entertainment center; the amusement park was scheduled to open the following spring.

Roberts elaborated: "It's incredibly historic property. The English first set foot on it thirteen years before the Mayflower docked at Plymouth Rock, even before they'd reached Jamestown. There are ruins of old plantations and trenches lacing the site that were used during both the Revolutionary and Civil Wars. We bought the land from Colonial Williamsburg. Some of the bluebloods over there wanted no part of us. They were afraid we'd defile their sacred restoration, but the local (James City County) economy and tax base is ailing, so Governor Rockefeller, who chairs the Colonial Williamsburg Foundation, thought we'd be a great addition to the area. But we have to get it right—critically and commercially. The master plan for the property is amazing. So we need to keep the wolves at bay while Joe Six-Pack and his family have a great time and spend lots of money at Busch Gardens. If we do, it'd be a real shot in the arm for tourism in that part of Virginia." (The Rockefeller in question was the erstwhile Winthrop, governor of Arkansas, whose family poured tens of millions into Williamsburg over the decades, making it the premier shrine to American colonial life and an honest-to-goodness national treasure.)

I saw it as both daunting and a huge opportunity. "We can leverage those assets," I declared after touring the site. "Only an Anheuser-Busch with its reputation for quality and vaunted reverence for history and tradition could attempt something like this—putting roller coasters next to a hallowed shrine like Colonial Williamsburg." Then I got busy. Since our firm still had no branch offices at that point, I recruited a network of affiliate agencies in key media centers—Betty Marshall in New York; David Swanston in Washington, DC; and Bob Thomas in Los Angeles. As I saw it, the key was to hire smallish agencies that would give our business top priority. (Proving that ignorance can indeed be blissful, I wasn't going to be concerned or held back by a little thing like zero knowledge or experience in the supremely relevant travel, tourism, or family entertainment areas of our business—a deficiency Monty Roberts seemed all too happy to overlook.)

So plunge ahead we did. Relying mostly on collective experience, instinct, and common sense, not to mention creativity, we developed a detailed master plan to publicize the Williamsburg venture. Preview briefings for news media were conducted in New York and Washington onboard the Anheuser-Busch yacht, the *A & Eagle*, a magnificent 119-foot German-built craft that wowed reporters and helped convey the notion that the Williamsburg project would be truly exceptional. We organized familiarization visits to the site using corporate aircraft to ferry journalists from key markets to Williamsburg. And we flew local Virginia officials to Saint Louis to tour the company's headquarters complex, which with three National Historic Landmark buildings looked as much like a wing of the Smithsonian Institution as a working brewery. Unpredictable and with boundless energy and seemingly insatiable appetites for women and spirits, Monty Roberts fancied himself, with some justification, as a creative impresario. Fickle and borderline manic, he was forever falling in and out of love with this girl or that or, figuratively speaking, with an endless succession of creative types—copy writers, art and film directors, voice-over talent, commercial actors, and the like. While the Williamsburg park was still under construction, Roberts had Gardner, his advertising agency, produce a television commercial to promote its nighttime hours. They decided to film it in the not-quite-complete German section; however, to make it happen the contractor had to bring in special high-intensity lighting. Arrangements were made for several of the rides to be working weeks before the park's opening, and a German band and dancers and a host of extras were hired to add authenticity and atmosphere to the scene. Compounding the challenge, the entire ad had to be shot in one evening.

In his capacity as executive producer of the shoot, from 9:00 p.m. to just before dawn the following morning Roberts slyly swilled vodka from a thermos and prowled the set, stopping occasionally to confer with the director about one thing or another and to ogle female cast members. I turned in early that evening and arrived back at the site at daybreak to fetch Roberts for breakfast. The two of us were walking out of the park as one of the German dancers—a voluptuous blonde—said, "Long night, huh, Mr. Roberts?"

"Yeah," he replied, "and you're about the only thing here that I haven't yet ridden."

Sixteen

Monty Roberts also was connected, and I was all too happy to ride those coattails.

Several weeks before the Williamsburg park opened, calling on some of Roberts's old automotive world contacts, we staged a twenty-four-hour endurance race with scaled-down replicas of vintage European racecars on the LeMans track in the French section of the attraction. We lined up student teams from the University of Maryland and the College of William & Mary to drive the vehicles, gas-powered putt-putts resembling antique go-carts, around the clock through a biting rain and wind. To spice up the weekend and attract media coverage, Roberts brought in some old cronies from his Detroit days: legendary car builder, racer, and gourmet chili baron Carroll Shelby; Phil Hill, the first and only American-born Formula One champion; 1925 Indianapolis 500 winner Peter DePaolo; the designer of the original Corvette, Zora Arkus-Duntoff, and a couple of other old-timers. They were automotive world icons, and I loved rubbing shoulders with them. As car guys in no time they removed the governors from the engines of their vehicles and staged their own five-lap "legends" event. Shelby cooked his famous chili for the college kids. However, DePaolo, by then an octogenarian, lost control of his car and it jumped an embankment and rammed into a retaining wall. The steering wheel impact badly bruised his chest, eliminating him from the competition and almost from the ranks of the living.

(The LeMans event was Monty Roberts's idea; the staging and media coverage pieces fell to me. But I vowed then and there that from that point forward we, the agency, would take the lead in originating ideas for newsworthy promotional strategies and events. There would be many, many of them in the years ahead.)

• • •

On the Saturday evening of the LeMans event weekend we hosted the auto world legends at a lavish private dinner at one of Williamsburg's charming colonial taverns. As desert and after-dinner drinks were served, Carroll Shelby rose and began reading passages from a Jack Daniels booklet on home medical cures—all of which involved liberal doses of the famed Tennessee sipping whiskey. His interpretation of the contents had us rolling in laughter. Afterward, Shelby, our West Coast PR affiliate Bob Thomas, and I closed our hotel bar. It was nearing 3:00 a.m., and we were feeling no pain as we boarded the elevator to finally turn in for the night. When we got to my floor, Thomas playfully put me in a bear hug and tried to prevent me from getting off the elevator. Somehow I was able to free my arms enough to give him a shot with both elbows, accidentally cracking a couple of his ribs.

Cracked ribs and steering wheel-caused contusions or not, the weekend was a major success. The Tidewater news media devoured the event. Monty Roberts and the powers-that-be back in Saint Louis were delighted, and to say that I was heady with the outcome was an understatement. I couldn't wait for the park's grand opening, which was just a month away!

Seventeen

"It wouldn't dare rain on Anheuser-Busch," invoked one of the company's special event coordinators as my sphincter muscles tightened. Nevertheless May 16, 1975, dawned ugly—cold, dark, raw, and rainy. So August Busch III, drawing on his well-honed agnostic instincts, opened the festivities with a special supplication: "Governor Godwin, honored excellencies, Mr. Busch Jr. and Mother Nature…"For the grand opening of the Williamsburg theme park, we cooked up a spectacular preview party and pageant to showcase the attraction to eight thousand invited VIPs—politicians, tourism officials, civic leaders, news media, and others. We brought in Ed McMahon, the affable *Tonight Show* second banana to Johnny Carson and a long-time spokesman for Budweiser, to serve as master of ceremonies. Old August Busch Jr. looked on as his son, McMahon, and Virginia Governor Miles Godwin, together with the English, French, and German ambassadors to the United States, christened each section of the park—riding the rides, tasting the food, and pronouncing the facility fit for public consumption. *Panorama,* a popular midday Washington TV talk show hosted back then by Maury Povich, originated live from the park. Travel and feature writers endorsed the attraction as far more than a traditional theme park. Wolf Von Eckardt, the *Washington Post*'s influential architecture and urban design critic, hailed it as a triumphant mixture of fun and enlightened land use, validating our early strategic assumptions and quieting the snooty National Geographic Society and Smithsonian types who ran Colonial Williamsburg and who'd initially opposed the venture. The rain held off for three hours—exactly the time it took to complete the formalities, giving me a perfect opportunity to hustle Busch III indoors for an interview we'd arranged for him with *Fortune* magazine.

The festivities were entirely our production, and Busch Gardens "The Old Country" opened to the general public the next day; by then the weather was perfect and thirty-five thousand paid their way into the facility, designed to accommodate twenty thousand. The Busches were ecstatic.

I was now certifiably hot stuff, and my life would never be the same.

• • •

Certain he was leading me swiftly down a path to perdition, Kathy Finnigan loathed Monty Roberts, feelings she did not try to hide. "Oh, he's all right," I tried to assure her, wondering if she'd been spooked by his booze-addled lecherous leering and certain she'd been offended by his brusque manners. "He needs me and a couple of other guys as a buffer. Granted he's loco, but I can learn a lot from him; he's the most creative, big thinker I've ever been around. I just have to be careful not to get swept up in the insanity."

Eighteen

In the mid-1950s, the exponentially growing number of Americans with television sets discovered a new way to wake up as NBC premiered the *Today Show.* The original host was an avuncular, soft-spoken bow-tie-wearing fellow by the name of Dave Garroway. He was supported by a cast of regulars, the best-known and most popular being a chimpanzee by the name of J. Fred Muggs.

Smart and initially well-mannered and loveable, Muggs cohosted the program with Garroway for nearly five years, delighting audiences with his antics until one day he bit a chunk out of the face of news anchor Frank Blair. Then Muggs's owners, former NBC pages Buddy Menella and Roy Waldron, moved to Tampa and signed on with African-themed Busch Gardens. Their aging, increasingly irascible meal ticket would do two performances daily in one of the theme park's open-air theaters.

Muggs also starred in a hysterical television commercial in which he parodied the iconic soliloquy from the movie *Patton.* Clad top to toenails in shocking pink satin plus fours, combat boots, a shirt-waist Eisenhower-style jacket, and matching helmet, he stood in front of an American flag, waved a riding crop, and moved his lips while a synchronized George C. Scott–like voice commanded viewers to visit Busch Gardens and have a good time. During the filming, Muggs became agitated and attacked the director of the TV spot, tearing a piece out of his rear end.

Muggs was still headlining at Busch Gardens when he reached the ripe old age of twenty-five, rare if not unheard of for a performing simian. Hoping the statute of limitations had expired on the transgression that led to his sudden departure from New York and NBC, I thought it might be time for the monkey to make a triumphant return to the Big Apple for a birthday celebration. It was risky, but worth trying.

We arranged with Eastern Airlines to provide transportation, removing a row of seats so his cage could fit in the first class section of the airplane. The late Thom Stork, then the capable Busch Gardens-Tampa resident PR person, would chaperone and coordinate the trip. The *Today Show* declined an offer to welcome Muggs back, but ABC's popular *Good Morning America* was delighted to book him.

Upon arriving at Marriott's Essex House Hotel, Muggs was scheduled to conduct a press conference. Exhausted from his travels, he waddled into the room, put his head down on a table, and appeared to doze off. However, when a *New York Times* photojournalist got too close, Muggs sprang to life and clobbered her with his powerful, telescopic arm, sending the photographer and her camera sprawling. Fortunately, she was not hurt, her camera still worked, and Muggs was on his best behavior for the *GMA* appearance the next day.

• • •

At about the same time the Tampa Busch Gardens installed a new coaster ride. It was called The Python in keeping with the park's African jungle motif and the ride's serpentine configuration. Before it opened to the public we staged a preview party for VIPs and news media. The city editor of the *Tampa Tribune* was among the riders. He was a well-liked fellow with a history of heart problems who was easily one hundred pounds overweight. After his ride he took about ten steps, sat down on the nearby bench, and expired. The theme for the ad campaign heralding the new ride was "Challenge the Python and Live." Monty Roberts called and asked me if the commercials should be suspended or scrapped given the newspaperman's death and, ever the risk-taker, I said, "Hell no, it will only add to the ride's mystique." The commercials continued to play, amazingly there was no negative outcry, and record throngs showed up to see what the new lethal contraption was all about.

• • •

Believing in the importance and impact of compelling visual images to convey the excitement and beauty of the Busch theme parks, I contracted with a succession of big-name, award-winning photographers to take pictures of the attractions.

For openers I turned David Hume Kennerly loose in Williamsburg and Tampa. The Pulitzer Prize winner and former official White House photographer got some great images. In Tampa, however, he brought the operations to a standstill a couple of times before going AWOL, having been enticed by a comely belly dancing snake charmer. “If you don’t get this camera guy under control fast I’m going to ban him from this place permanently,” threatened the park’s general manager. “What can I say? He’s an artiste,” I countered while scrambling to reach and rein in the frisky lensman to whom I’d paid a hefty sum for the rights to get his work and the use of his name and images.

Nineteen

With early success came advancement—promotion to vice president and partner at Fleishman-Hillard—along with more income, more responsibility, and an opportunity to own stock in the firm. And, sure enough, theme parks would prove to be child's play (lame pun intended) compared with what was to come next. It was at about that time that I got another call from Denny Long, who said he soon expected to be named president of Anheuser-Busch, Inc., responsible for the company's beer business, the mother cow that accounted for 90 percent of its sales and profits. "Given your resounding Busch Gardens successes, we need you to do for the beer division what you've been doing for the theme parks," he said.

I advised Long that—no surprise—a program for the beer company would need to be much larger and more comprehensive in scope, requiring added PR people in more key cities and a much larger budget. Then I shared the news with John Graham. "This is exactly the break we need. If we do it right, Fleishman-Hillard can become a major player in this industry," he predicted.

We then regaled Busch III and Long with a concept for a long-range vision for the company: to give consumers, investors, distributors, and employees a sense of what I termed "the mystical body of Anheuser-Busch," no blasphemy intended. "Given the company's history and traditions, its reputation for quality, the rich imagery already in place, and the manner in which we touch the lives of millions of people with our products, programs, and messages, we can foster a feeling of almost religious kinship for the company. No other brewer can do that." They grasped the idea quickly and heartily endorsed it.

At roughly the same time, Anheuser-Busch was feeling mounting pressure from the barons of Wall Street and two competitors, Joseph Schlitz and Miller Brewing. Investors were growing impatient because while A-B continued to lead the industry in sales, its profits were being squeezed by the spiraling costs of agricultural ingredients, packaging materials, and energy. Old Gussie Busch, still in charge, vowed the company would never compromise on the quality of its products with cheaper ingredients or a shorter brewing cycle. Instead he furloughed two hundred white-collar employees, most of them middle managers in sales and marketing. Dick Meyer, by then the company's president, resigned in protest, paving the way for the ascension of Denny Long.

Meanwhile Schlitz, a.k.a. "The Beer That Made Milwaukee Famous," and number two in industry sales at the time and gaining, posted dramatically improved earnings. Its stock price began to climb, generating positive interest on Wall Street and in the business and financial media. Then Schlitz Chairman Robert Uihlein boasted in *Business Week* that his company's enhanced performance was due largely to the use of new technology that hastened the brewing cycle by pumping artificial carbonation into the liquid rather than allowing it to age naturally. The article made note of the fact that Busch Jr. had resisted such innovation, inferring he would rather opt for superior quality, and insisting that over the long haul beer drinkers would be able to tell the difference. Uihlein boasted that Schlitz could now be made in fifteen days; it still took forty days to brew Budweiser.

Seeing that in print, I couldn't believe my eyes. We had the article reproduced, highlighting the Uihlein quote, which credited agitated batch fermentation and the injection of bottled carbon dioxide for the brewing cycle speedup that accounted for the Schlitz profitability rebound. Hundreds of thousands of copies of the story found their way to the beer drinking public. In less than a year, the Schlitz threat had passed, due largely to the self-incriminating remarks of the company's chairman and the decisive actions of our Anheuser-Busch PR apparatus. It was in a sense the Fort Sumter of the industry era that came to be known as Beer Wars. And for me the idea of using communications to commit guerrilla warfare was a major turn-on. I relished playing the role of the Anheuser-Busch attack dog.

• • •

I found myself spending more and more time working directly with Long and Busch III, who finally had unseated his father as CEO in a palace coup that resulted in bad blood between father and son. August, as he insisted on being called, was savvy, ruthless, and trusting of almost no one. He had a permanent chip on his shoulder and a go-for-the-jugular approach to business and the competition, which I admired greatly.

The fourth generation of his family to preside over the empire begun in the 1860s by his great-grandfather, Adolphus, and the third of eleven of prolific Gussie's children by three of his four wives, Busch III was a recovering playboy whose management style involved a combination of hard work, uncanny instinct, unparalleled industry knowledge, and calculated intimidation, perhaps employed to compensate for his prodigal past and to impress his larger than life father, who in better times he called Chief.

Severely handsome and almost irrationally intense, young August's most lethal weapon was piercing blue eyes that seemed to pop out of their sockets when he got angry or sought to emphasize something. He left college in Arizona after a couple of inconclusive years, earned a diploma in brewing science from Chicago's Siebel Institute, and then joined the union and worked as a brewery laborer before beginning his climb through the managerial ranks. He was an accomplished aviator, tennis player, and an avid rod and gun outdoorsman. A divorced father of two in his midthirties, he was one of America's most eligible bachelors when I started working with him. (A couple of years later he would remarry, exchanging vows in Cabo San Lucas, Mexico, with a beautiful and brainy blonde, Virginia Lee Wiley, who hailed from Buffalo, New York. They remain married today.)

Sensing opportunity, we began beefing up the Fleishman-Hillard talent pool, recruiting a brigade of bright, young ragtag communicators with energy, ideas, and entrepreneurial spirit to burn but almost no formal public relations or managerial experience. Together over the next twenty years they would form the nucleus that began to propel the agency to national and, ultimately, international prominence. We were cooking!

At the same time I became a virtual embed at the brewery, with an assigned office, company health club privileges, access to the executive dining room, the works. My time was 100 percent dedicated to the company; I was high-profile on-site most of the time, making me the first F-H person to be on staff with a client—a practice that in time became much more common in our business.

Twenty

The Miller threat was far more formidable and potentially lethal than that from Schlitz. And in the wake of our beat-down of the Schlitz attempted encroachment, pressure was mounting on those of us on the PR side to do something about it. Philip Morris, Inc., had acquired Miller, which meant a huge infusion of marketing savvy and money, but—and this would prove key—almost no adult beverage experience. With tobacco-bred leadership and budget to burn, Miller successfully introduced a new, lower-calorie light beer, revitalized its flagship High Life brand, and forged an exclusive US relationship with the great German brewer Lowenbrau. Suddenly, the long-slumbering brewing industry was shaken from its footings, prompting Miller CEO John Murphy to predict "it's not a question of whether but when" they knocked Anheuser-Busch from its industry leading perch. Murphy reportedly kept an August Busch III voodoo doll in his office and delighted in sticking pins into it while wiping his feet on a rug bearing the company's iconic A & Eagle logo. Journalists covering the growing hostilities between the two brewers were quick to chronicle Murphy's antics. And Denny Long made sure clippings of those stories were just as quickly posted on the bulletin boards and employee lockers at Anheuser-Busch.

Miller fired an early Beer Wars salvo challenging the Anheuser-Busch claim that its products were brewed with all-natural ingredients since tannin, a chemical, could be found in its products. "Simple," came our response, "tannin occurs naturally in our beers as a by-product of the brewing process." Anheuser-Busch called the attack "a low blow and sour grapes" by a competitor who couldn't make the same claim due to its use of foam enhancers, preservatives, artificial flavoring, and antioxidants (all supposedly needed because of Miller's clear bottle). Then Miller took a shot at Anheuser's vaunted beechwood aging process, dismissing it as nothing more than "the dumping of chemically treated slats into the ageing tanks."

"Tell Philip Morris to come right along, and tell them to bring their money," Busch III responded with characteristic machismo via a *Business Week* article—fighting words he confided later to me that he hoped he wouldn't have to eat given the depth of the rival's pockets. (He refused to call Miller by its given name, opting instead to use what he considered the more pejorative reference, never missing an opportunity to link the rival brewery with its tobacco conglomerate ownership.)

Just as Miller was making its move, Anheuser-Busch's contracts with its labor unions expired. Negotiations bogged down. A strike date was set, and the hourly workers walked out of all ten breweries in March, a key inventory-building period for the coming summer peak beer-drinking season. Rather than shut down, the company elected to operate using nonunion, supervisory personnel who were physically unaccustomed to and operationally unfamiliar with the rigors of brewing, packaging, and shipping. Production fell by at least 50 percent; sales and market share followed suit.

Things got ugly. In Saint Louis, several hundred hourly workers armed with baseball bats assembled at 3:00 a.m. in Lyons Park near the brewery and began breaking the windows of cars belonging to people working in the nearby bottling plant. When the police arrived, the union leaders said they were just getting ready to play a ballgame. In Jacksonville, Florida, trucks entering and exiting the plant were shot at from a nearby wooded area by an unknown rifleman. In that case, to regain some share of voice as much as anything, we offered a cash reward for information leading to the apprehension of the perpetrators. Loathe to negotiate through the news media, there was little we would do or say publicly during the work stoppage, but I was on duty to field media inquiries and, in limited instances, respond to union allegations. An agreement was finally reached in early June after one hundred days; the impact was devastating in terms of lost distribution, sales, and competitive momentum.

The strike was a call to arms for Anheuser-Busch. The company saw itself at war, and Dennis Long was the three-star general in command of the all-out mobilization, calling the shots from a war room set up down the hall from his office. Older executives were reassigned to less critical jobs or replaced outright with younger ones. Brand management was reintroduced around a bevy of best and brightest MBAs recruited from the top consumer package goods companies, almost all of them graduates of elite business schools. New products, packages, and advertising campaigns were launched and millions upon millions of dollars' worth of paid media and special events were purchased, including sponsorship of a staggering array of professional and college sports broadcasts. For the first time, beer and speed were no longer taboo together as the company embarked on sponsorships of NASCAR and Indy Car teams. The battle cry was "A Sense of Urgency." Legions of hourly workers back on the job sported "Miller Killer" tee shirts. And at Fleishman-Hillard we rolled out a massive program to provide aggressive PR support for the initiative. John Graham was by then the agency's president and chief operating officer; at age thirty-two I was promoted to executive vice president and senior partner, making me the agency's first-ever EVP.

Confident the dramatic infusion of new programs, sponsorships, and people would soon yield tangible results, Long asked presciently, "How can we use PR to leverage the momentum that is sure to come?" So my beer team devised a method to publicize sales gains by each Anheuser-Busch product every three months, state by state. The quarterly performance initiative, as it was known internally, was extremely effective and paid extra dividends in the form of morale boosts with the company's vast network of local wholesale distributors and its field sales force while impressing retailers in the many states where the increases were being achieved.

Twenty-One

One commercial property Anheuser-Busch could not acquire at the time was *Monday Night Football*, ABC-TV's immensely popular new NFL extravaganza, which Miller had locked up with an exclusive long-term deal. So the brewery did the next best thing: it acquired rights to the *radio* broadcasts of the Monday night games featuring announcers Jack Buck and Hank Stram, former Super Bowl-winning coach of the Kansas City Chiefs. To promote the ad buy to distributors and retailers, the Budweiser brand team bought thousands of bright red battery-powered transistor radios shaped like miniature football helmets sporting the brand's familiar bow tie logo.

That gave me an idea. I whipped up a news release in which the company's newly named marketing vice president, Michael Roarty, was quoted urging fans to watch the Monday night telecasts but to mute the TV audio and listen to the radio accounts of the games. It was delivered to journalists accompanied by dozens of the little red helmet radios and included the claim that Anheuser-Busch market research revealed that Monday night football audiences preferred Buck and Stram to the annoying television riffs and rants of ABC's Howard Cosell.

The subsequent news coverage scored a direct hit. Cosell came unglued. His colossal ego wounded, he called Roarty, demanded to see the research, and threatened to sue Anheuser-Busch.

"What are we going to do about this?" the conflict-averse Roarty asked me with Cosell parked on hold on another phone line.

"Make sure he has your correct address so he can serve the papers, and tell him we'll see him in court; he's playing right into our hands," I advised. "Cosell is one of those shrill, sanctimonious public figures the news media and sports fans love to hate. We were banking on that all along."

That ended the matter then and there, and listenership of the Monday night radio broadcasts reached an all-time high, thanks in part to our calculated promotion, and Mike Roarty was both delighted and relieved.

• • •

Not long after the labor settlement, *Forbes,* the influential business magazine, published an article claiming A-B was still in deep trouble—that it couldn't shake the effects of the prolonged work stoppage or withstand the onslaught of Miller's marketing mojo. Illustrated with a Budweiser bottle covered with cobwebs, the story laid blame on patriarch Gussie Busch who, it suggested, was too old-school and tradition-bound to compete in the modern era. It paid little heed to the fact that Busch III was by then in charge (and had been for several years) and that the brewery's recent "all in" initiatives were beginning to bear fruit, information that was readily available from any number of independent, well-informed industry analysts. Instead it unfairly took to task the aging baron, who ironically had been hailed as the foremost innovator of the previous industry generation.

The article hurt the old man and Busch III deeply, and the son declared an embargo against further cooperation with the magazine. To me, the knee-jerk reaction to the *Forbes* piece was understandable but disconcerting given the publication's prominence and the reality that with or without a given company's cooperation, the magazine would be published each week and would continue to cover A-B and the beer industry. The decision was a mistake, but Busch III was not to be dissuaded, so stubborn was his spirit and so deeply ingrained his mistrust of the news media. Little did I realize at the time how ultimately his decree would come to affect me personally.

• • •

Gardner, the advertising agency of record for Busch Beer and Busch Gardens, was acquired at about that time by Wells, Rich & Greene, one of the highest of the high flyers on Madison Avenue. Wells, Rich also had a sizable chunk of Philip Morris's cigarette business, but did not handle the Miller Brewing account. Busch III nevertheless chose to view that as a conflict and told Mary Wells that unless she divested her agency of its tobacco accounts the Busch Beer and Busch Gardens business would go elsewhere. Ms. Wells didn't blink, nor did Mr. Busch, and that was that. The beer account went to Needham, Harper & Steers (now DDB Needham) in Chicago, and the Busch Gardens business to McDonald & Little in Atlanta. Gardner's days as an agency thus were numbered.

Twenty-Two

"Holy shit! Ain't no way I'm riding that thing!" exclaimed "Mean Joe" Greene upon getting his first look at the new roller coaster at three-year-old Busch Gardens in Williamsburg.

Greene, the imposing Pittsburgh Steelers All-Pro lineman and a member of the famed Steel Curtain defense, was one of the "eight bravest and/or meanest people in the world" we brought in to christen the sadistic new contraption. Hailed as the scariest, fastest steel coaster on earth, it was called the Loch Ness Monster, partly because of its diabolic, serpentine configuration and partly because it stretched above the tree line in the Scottish section of the park, its longest drop bottoming out just above a looming lake that was, of course, dubbed Loch Ness.

A portion of the ride traveled through a pitch dark zone. When we set out to do a test run a day or two before the official inaugural ride, August A. Busch III insisted that we light that section before he would take the ride—believe it or not. It turned out that this otherwise swashbuckling jet plane and helicopter pilot had a phobia about tight, dark places, so Harold Greenblatt, the park's engineer, arranged to have strands of Christmas lights strung throughout the dark section—solely for the test ride and the opening day festivities.

The idea for the stunt grew out of my friendship with Conrad Dobler, an All-Pro offensive guard for the Saint Louis Football Cardinals (now the Arizona Cardinals), who back then was reputed to be NFL's dirtiest player. Dobler and Greene, who as it turned out was mortally afraid of heights and roller coasters, were joined by hearing-impaired movie stuntwoman Kitty O'Neill; race car driver Janet Guthrie, the first woman to compete in the Indianapolis 500; daredevil George Willig, who famously scaled to the top of the late, lamented World Trade Center, and three other notable brave hearts who together would take the inaugural ride along with Busch III. Despite his hesitance, goaded by Major, his ten-year-old son, Greene rode it anyway, and it was a colossal success capped off by a three-and-a-half minute segment on Walter Cronkite's *CBS Evening News.* The network correspondent who covered the event got caught up in the moment and declared that it was one of the most imaginative publicity stunts he'd ever encountered. "It transcends hype; it's legitimate news," he declared. I knew better, but who was I to differ with a network correspondent?

A week later, we arranged a visit by Alex Campbell, an octogenarian from a small Scottish village on the banks of the real Loch Ness who in all seriousness claimed to have seen the actual monster more times than any other living person—a claim that was more or less confirmed by National Geographic magazine. Mr. Campbell, who had not visited the United States before, brought along a vial of water from the legendary lake to baptize the ride and bring good fortune to all who braved it.

Twenty-Three

To me the take-no-prisoners climate at Anheuser-Busch was both exhilarating and addictive. The testosterone level was almost visible to the naked eye. It started at the top and flowed down through the food chain, creating a highly charged all-macho-all-the-time atmosphere in which barbaric behavior and its stepchild fear were commonplace. Requests were seldom made; instead commands were issued. Fools were not suffered, nor were delays, indecision, or what the chieftains considered to be phony intellectualism. It was a power trip all the way, and I learned to play the game quickly and expertly, especially around the offices of Fleishman-Hillard where my fair-haired-boy status seemed a license to plunder. If John Graham received complaints about my sometimes boorish slash-and-burn style, they were largely overlooked, perhaps because of a strong sense of looming opportunity within the agency, spawned of course by our steadily expanding relationship with the brewery as well as my apparent (to that point in time) charmed touch.

My seeming immunity to adhering to conventional norms of conduct within my own organization may also have been due to widespread recognition that I was working without a proverbial net above the chum-filled waters ever swirling around the brewery's newly crowned emperor, August A. Busch III. Look at the man the wrong way or say the wrong thing to him and it was off with your head. It was daunting enough for Busch's own employees, but the risk factor increased exponentially for me; not only was I the company's principal mouthpiece, I was also an outsider, an agency person, whose every utterance was subject to microscopic scrutiny and second-guessing, if not condemnation. And sooner or later agency people were all too often expendable. Few had the asbestos-clad psyches to play that role. I found it intoxicating.

In time, we came to understand our firm's potential and saw clearly a path to destiny. "We can ride this horse a long way," I suggested to Graham on a flight to the West Coast as we scribbled an outline of our vision for growth on a cocktail napkin, "except ours just happens to be an eight-horse Clydesdale hitch rather than a lone steed." Soon we parlayed our newfound success into an honest-to-goodness national presence. Brewery business helped us bankroll new branch offices in New York and Los Angeles, replacing capable, independent affiliate agencies in those locations with our own operations. At the same time, thanks to the fresh talent we'd recruited, growing client needs, and confidence in our capabilities, the Anheuser-Busch business expanded beyond beer and family entertainment to include industry and public affairs and a variety of other specialty areas. We were on a roll!

• • •

In 1977 Fleishman-Hillard bracketed its presence in the State of Missouri, opening a Kansas City office when the indomitable Betsey Solberg agreed to throw in with us and create a permanent presence there. The Kansas City office was an immediate success, and its launch went so smoothly that we may have had a false sense of security when, in 1980, it came time to make our next move—the Big Apple.

Our initial choice for general manager of the New York operation was an erstwhile Englishman who'd cut his teeth on Fleet Street before moving to the colonies, and he was a disaster. Fortunately we'd propped him up with two young account executives—Wayne Charness and Karen Teitelbaum—both of whom had worked for and with me previously and were capable and trustworthy.

One day as I was working away in my Saint Louis office the phone rang. Karen Teitelbaum was on the line, and she was hyperventilating. "You've got to stop him," she cried, and went on to explain that the GM was in the process of pitching a *Wall Street Journal* reporter on a story based on the findings of a topical survey that he claimed had been conducted on behalf of one of his clients. The problem was that no such survey had been conducted; the entire thing was a hoax, and he had cooked up some bogus results. I told Graham what was happening, and he got on the phone with the fellow and instructed him to put an end to the ruse or face immediate termination. The handwriting was on the wall with that man anyway, and a short time later he got his walking papers.

As time went by we established successful operations around relatively solid leadership in Los Angeles, Washington, DC, and Chicago, but encountered other fits and starts elsewhere in the United States, Europe, and Asia—eventually ironing out those kinks en route to national and eventually international expansion and prominence. Nevertheless, New York and a handful of other early experiences provided valuable lessons, to wit: that we needed to be more thorough in vetting key candidates, and that the PR business had its share of frauds and rascals at every level.

Twenty-Four

One evening after dinner following a planning meeting at a Lake of the Ozarks resort, Denny Long invited me to go for a walk. "August really likes you," Long said as we strolled the grounds. "He likes your focus and creativity, and he wants you to come to work for us."

Of course I was genuinely flattered. On the one hand I both looked up to Busch III and felt tremendous loyalty to him. On the other I had more than a healthy dose of fear of him. And I believed fervently in what at the time Graham and I were trying to achieve—growing our firm to be a major player in the communications consulting business—and that if anything were to happen to my or the agency's relationship with the brewery, as a partner in the firm hopefully I could work for other F-H clients, although my heart, soul, and ego were completely invested in the A-B business. At the same time my instincts suggested that I might not be as effective in a freedom-choking, structured corporate environment considering the size, volatility, hierarchy, and politics of A-B. Besides, the prevailing entrepreneurial spirit at F-H was a siren call. Truth be told, the hired gun role suited me just fine, especially since our license to function was sanctioned by the very top people in the A-B organization, usually insulating us from those on the client side who might otherwise impede our ability to operate.

"I sincerely appreciate the offer," I told Long, "but I can do you and August more good where I am. I am one hundred percent dedicated to A-B, and we've put together an extraordinarily talented team of men and women to work on your business. It would be virtually impossible to replicate that expertise outside of an agency setting." Long and Busch accepted that response. It would ultimately turn out to be prescient.

• • •

Our ability to function smoothly at Anheuser-Busch was due to a unique combination of factors. First, the company had no *external* PR function. We were it, and we did it all—media relations; reputation management; corporate and financial communications; troubleshooting, including occasional mud-slinging and crisis work; marketing, promotional, and special event support, you name it. Second, we were employed and thus chartered by those at the highest levels of the company—the chairman, vice chairman, and president of the organization. Our bills went to them, and our power, influence, and charter to operate derived from them, giving us exceptional, unfettered access and maneuverability. The rest of the organization knew that and accepted, or perhaps even welcomed it, and understood from whom and whence we came. And third, we did an extraordinarily good job for them—a job that has not been equaled since the company took the PR function in-house in the latter half of the '90s, which was due to Busch III's distrust of everyone and everything and his growing need to control those who served him.

Twenty-Five

Our offices were still in the CBS Building (One Memorial Drive) when one day I returned from a client meeting and almost literally tripped over five or six freelance graphic designers in our reception lobby. That prompted me to ask our accounting department how much we were paying outside contractors for our design work—virtually all of it on behalf of paying clients. After a quick study they reported that in the previous twelve months we'd paid these vendors more than a million dollars! That was big money for a fast-rising agency in the early 1980s.

I took that information to John Graham and said, "We are missing the boat. We should establish our own design capability, capture a share of that revenue, and have better control over the finished work product, benefiting us and our clients."

Graham seemed equally surprised and intrigued. The idea met momentarily and inexplicably with resistance from one of the partners, but I held fast to the idea, was able to generate support from a number of other partners, and before long was proceeding to make the idea a reality.

In short order we recruited several talented designers to form the nucleus of a first-rate department. At its peak several years ago, that business unit flourished, employing sixty-five people and generating $13 million in annual revenue while turning out superb publications, websites, glitzy presentations, and a host of interactive products.

(Strapped for space, in 1985 the firm moved its headquarters from the Gateway Tower building at One Memorial Drive to Saint Louis Place, a brand-new building at the corner of Pine and Broadway, where ultimately the agency would occupy a half dozen floors comprising more than 150,000 square feet. At that point it was believed to be one of the world's largest civilian public relations installations under one roof. The firm remains there to this day.)

• • •

I was a better provider than parent, and things were not so rosy on the home front. My sons—by then three in number with the birth of Patrick—were growing up and starting school, but I was too wrapped up in my work and other forms of self-absorption and gratification to provide enough of the fatherly attention they needed and deserved at that age. I was too quick to snap at them and too slow to nurture. They were bright, cute, and funny little fellows, and Kathy all too often had to make excuses for me. "Your daddy's tired. Your daddy has work to do. Your daddy's expecting an important phone call." Whatever at the time seemed to fit. It was never, "Your daddy's too self-important" or "Your daddy's had too much to drink," which was increasingly the case, never mind that growing up I'd never received much in the way of proper fathering. I loved them dearly, but didn't always know how to show it. And Kathy, while ever the enabler and a true master of the motherly arts, grew increasingly frustrated and angry at my delinquency, which extended both to her and our boys.

• • •

Things were moving fast. I was promoted to executive vice president and senior partner, the first in the agency's history to hold that title. I thought I was bulletproof. I got a vanity license plate for my flashy new white Buick Rivera Buick convertible. "Hype" it read, and off I rode to become master of the universe. What I soon discovered was that with that car and that plate seemingly everyone in town knew where I was at almost every given moment. Pure hubris.

Twenty-Six

On a roll with its High Life and Miller Lite successes, Miller Brewing began distributing the renowned German beer Lowenbrau in the United States. In those days Lowenbrau probably was as well-known and popular in the US import category as Heineken. A brilliant and hefty $35 million advertising campaign themed "Let it be Lowenbrau" supported the introduction. Elegant, rich-textured television commercials featured evocative original theme music with vocals by throaty jazz and blues legend Arthur Prysock. European imports were gaining in popularity in the United States at the time, and Miller was out in front of the curve with Lowenbrau, or so it appeared. (At the time Anheuser-Busch did not have an entry in the import category; Michelob, a relatively full-bodied domestic super premium introduced in 1896, was its closest contender.)

Before long, however, Miller quietly switched a domestically produced version of Lowenbrau for the genuine original article. Instead of being brewed in Munich, the ersatz "import" was produced in local Miller breweries in the United States. The problem was that unless they used a magnifying glass to decipher the fine print on the label, consumers could not detect the difference, at least not until they tasted the product.

Coincidentally, I took a call about then from a *Forbes* reporter who said he was doing a story on the growing popularity of imported beers in America. "What about fake imports?" I asked, calculatedly ignoring the Busch III edict against dealing with that publication. The reporter bit, and I proceeded to provide him with background on the

Miller-Lowenbrau conspiracy. Anticipating this and other such opportunities, I had purchased a stash of original Munich-brewed Lowenbrau before it vanished from retail shelves altogether. I had a six-pack and a single bottle of the German product photographed, showing it and the virtually indistinguishable US version side-by-side and close up. I shipped a set of the photos, *unretouched* of course, and an actual six-pack of the original product to the *Forbes* writer, who turned out a story that caused heartburn for the big wigs in Milwaukee and Munich—and pure joy among their archrivals in Saint Louis. Our production room couldn't crank out the reprints fast enough.

The *Forbes* coup gave rise to another idea, a potential whopper. Summoning my inner pit bull, I dashed over to the office of Donald S. "Sandy" McDonald, the brewery's chief legal counsel and a trusted friend. (McDonald was an heir to the Liggett & Myers tobacco fortune, and as such felt beholden to no one.) We began by discussing the Miller/Lowenbrau situation in the context of the *Forbes* story. "We've got a live one here; why can't we file a lawsuit or get a court order to make them stop this bullshit?" I asked. "Because they're not doing anything illegal," McDonald cautioned. "They have a contract with Lowenbrau to do what they're doing—licensed brewing—and there's not a goddamn thing we can do about it," said the Ivy League-educated barrister. However, the more we talked the more riled up McDonald too became.

We placed an exploratory call to Terry Sheehy at Howery & Simon, one of the brewery's high-powered Washington, DC, law firms. We told him about the *Forbes* article and posed the question: "How can we drive a stake further into their scheming little black hearts? Goes to show you what happens when the cigarette boys get into the beer business; they'll stop at nothing, and they truly don't understand the beer drinker." After some give and take, Sheehy hit on the idea of filing a deceptive marketing practices complaint against Miller with the Federal Trade Commission. "Would something like this have traction?" he asked as I began to hyperventilate. "Does a bear shit in the woods?" I responded. "Seriously, if the complaint has substance and credibility, you bet it will," I said. "Here's the key: Lowenbrau is not aimed at your typical beer drinker. It's for the upscale, well-educated type who thinks of himself as a connoisseur. He of all people doesn't like to be ripped off or made to look foolish. He tends to be current on the news of the day; woe betide those who try to take advantage of him, and he has a very long memory."

"The FTC will never act on it," McDonald predicted.

"Not a problem," I replied. "We'll generate so much up front press coverage with this thing it won't matter. If we do it right we can annihilate this product—literally. We're talking about nothing less than the proverbial terrible swift sword here, boys."

We took the idea to Long and Busch III. In less than ten minutes we outlined the idea and the strategy behind it. "How soon can Sheehey have the complaint ready to go?" Long asked as he and Busch tried to disguise their glee.

A week or so later Sheehy was in Saint Louis with a draft of a proposed FTC filing. It was right on the mark, chock full of juicy, solid, sound-bite rhetoric and compelling visual exhibits. The eighty-page complaint was perfect for our purposes. Simultaneous with the FTC filing, Saint Louis and our coast-to-coast branch and affiliate offices released the contents of the document to dozens of news organizations.

Early on I heard from Steve Byers, the *Milwaukee Journal-Sentinel* business writer who covered the brewing industry. (Byers went on to teach journalism at my alma mater, Marquette.) "This was nothing more than a pissing contest until now," he said, "but it looks like you really got them this time. Their top brass is livid, and their PR people (Guy Smith and Ray Minkus) have come unhinged."

"Good," I replied. "Those sneaky bastards got exactly what they had coming."

The immediate news coverage was blockbuster and completely one-sided. Plus the move spawned a series of lethal aftershocks—indignant columns and editorials, threats by states attorneys general and other opportunistic consumer advocates to investigate the alleged Miller/Lowenbrau fraud, and various other reactions far beyond the expectations of Anheuser-Busch senior management and their PR brain trust. The capper came when John Cunniff, an Associated Press business columnist, managed to reach a Lowenbrau executive in Munich by phone and he expressed—*on-the-record*—his company's shock, anger, and disgrace, hinting their contractual agreement with Miller might be in peril.

Miller's response was anemic and predictable, dismissing the complaint as a competitively inspired ploy. In the hope of drowning out the controversy they intensified the Lowenbrau advertising level, but the substance and power of our motion was dramatic and virtually irrefutable. As expected, the FTC never did act on the complaint, and it didn't matter. Within six months it was almost impossible to find the product for sale in taverns and supermarkets, and before long its marketing support all but evaporated. For all intents and purposes, American-brewed Lowenbrau was history, and while our client didn't plan a ticker tape parade for us down Pestalozzi Street, which runs through the heart of the brewery, we were flying high! (The Miller-Lowenbrau relationship formally ended a short time later, much to the embarrassment of the great German brewer.)

I have often cited the anti-Lowenbrau attack as one of the highlights of my career at various seminars, college lectures, panel discussions, and other forums. Such situations don't present themselves all that often, but when they do, and if the guerrilla response is well planned and executed, the results can be exhilarating, measurable and devastating to the other side.

Twenty-Seven

Fleishman-Hillard was fast becoming a refuge of choice for talented communicators, especially newspaper reporters, those ink-stained wretches who wanted to break the vicious circle of their drab existence marked stereotypically by cussing, spitting, and endangering their livers at seedy saloons in some cases before, during, and after work. Now there was a real alternative: they could cuss, spit, and risk their organs in more gentrified, higher stakes surroundings. All they had to do was "sell out," to make the transition from journalism to agency life.

There was to that point at least one noteworthy blemish on our otherwise enviable recruiting record. This fellow's professional pedigree was superb. After serving as a speechwriter and press secretary for a Michigan governor, he went to work for the Sunday magazine of the *Free-Press,* Detroit's leading daily newspaper. He was an excellent writer with a finely honed wit. However, he proved to be slothful and pretentious—far more interested in the trappings and perks of agency life than the hard work needed to succeed in it.

He was part of my beer team assigned to the Michelob brand. In that capacity he was responsible for providing PR support for brand-sponsored special and sporting events—America's Cup yacht racing, polo, the PGA Tour, and various jazz and other upscale musical ventures. In time I became concerned because it seemed he was never reachable when I needed him, and despite plenty of imaginative excuses, he frequently missed deadlines and was too often observed behaving more like a client than an agency person.

Finally, I felt I could ill afford to be more tolerant of or patient with this bloke, and our relationship quickly frayed. Frustrated, I more than once accused him to his face of being lazy and disingenuous. With tensions rising between us, I was in my office one day with multiple plates spinning as usual when an interagency envelope marked "personal and confidential" landed on my desk. It contained a copy of a news release I'd written. This fellow had circled the opening paragraph and written a note in the margin: "Is not a complete sentence—does not contain a verb." Big mistake. I reviewed the paragraph in question and saw that its wording was acceptable and its meaning clear; I had merely elected to take some creative license with it. Then I took a deep breath and sent the document and this fellow's original comment back to him with a cover message that employed perhaps the most versatile, albeit crude, word in the English language:

"Fuck you, that is."

The next day he was shown the door.

• • •

Success does indeed breed success as the adage insists, and as F-H grew operationally and reputation-wise we were blessed to attract dozens of top-drawer talents to our ranks. Nevertheless, the PR business has its share of frauds and others who are simply out of their depth, and Fleishman-Hillard was and is not immune from that scourge. Yet the rascals and the disappointments, few though they were, remained on the margins; they could not overpower our momentum and the legion of talent we were able to attract over time. And it's fair to say that we learned from each and every one of those personnel mistakes.

• • •

I was hanging out during a Cardinals game one evening at the Redbird Roost, Gussie Busch's private box at Busch Stadium II. After downing a few cold, frosty ones I got into a spirited discussion with (the late) Jerry Clinton, a Saint Louis area beer wholesaler who'd also had several pops. He was whining about how difficult it was for him to do business with Busch III nearby and always watching his every move. "You poor SOB," I said facetiously, "what's your market share these days?" (I knew it was north of a whopping 70 percent.) "You asshole," he replied, "you're the only PR guy I know who needs a PR guy."

Twenty-Eight

August Busch III was obsessed with the idea of creating a soft drink for the adult market. His inspiration was a beverage popular in the United Kingdom called Shandy, essentially a blend of beer and lemonade. And when August was obsessed with something, nothing could stand in his way. Nothing.

Anheuser-Busch's flavor scientists believed that as consumers age they tend to lose their taste for traditional sweeter soft drinks. So they set out to create a nonalcoholic product for the mature palate using a malt base, carbonation, and lemon, apple, and ginger flavoring. The result was Chelsea, a pleasing but comparatively dry-tasting concoction that looked and foamed like beer but tasted something like ginger ale. It came in an elegant tapered clear glass bottle with sophisticated foil labeling.

The plan was to test market Chelsea in five locations with a slick advertising campaign touting it as the "Not So Soft Drink." Technically and legally, Chelsea was a soft drink, as it contained approximately 0.04 percent alcohol by volume, the threshold being 0.05 percent. But its beer-like appearance and advertising slogan, plus the fact that the world's largest brewer produced it, brought forth a firestorm of criticism from parents, health-care professionals, religious fundamentalists, and politicians in and around Richmond, Virginia, one of the test markets. They tagged it "Baby Beer" and claimed it was an attempt to introduce minors to a beer-like product, priming them to graduate eventually to the real thing. The other four test markets remained controversy free.

The uproar was patently ridiculous. It was inconceivable that Anheuser-Busch would risk its franchise with its loyal adult public, let alone its reputation as one of America's most admired, responsible, well-managed (and closely regulated) companies to take such a flier. Yet that is exactly what happened. If the company's public relations and marketing experts, myself included, sensed some concerns going into the test market, we failed to sound the alarm. We let ourselves get swept up in the excitement, not to mention the politics of the endeavor.

It fell to me and the Chelsea brand manager, a fellow named Keith Jones freshly recruited from Pepsi Cola, to save the day, but we discovered quickly and painfully that we could not fight rampant emotionalism, which begot a frenzy of media criticism, with fact and reason. The Chelsea test markets were discontinued. The product manager left the company. And the Anheuser-Busch senior executive responsible for new product development and diversification—a Wharton MBA who was yet to chaperone a success despite numerous previous forays with other soft drinks, snack foods, wine, and eventually international expansion—was quick to pin the debacle on our inability to stave off the wolves rather than an inherent flaw in the overall product concept.

Test markets, by definition, are intended to help distinguish those products with real potential for success and to ferret out the others. Hard to admit as it may have been, Chelsea was among the others. The mistake I made personally, and that we made as an agency, was not having better-honed antennae and not speaking up; there was so much hullabaloo surrounding Chelsea that politically it seemed clear such concerns would be unwelcome, the culture of silence and intimidation at A-B being what it was. Nevertheless, we were too close to the project to be objective; that can be fatal in our business.

It was the first major setback of my otherwise charmed agency career—to that point in time.

(Ironically, the adult beverage shelves today are full of lemon-based or flavored alcoholic beverages and they are controversy free. Variations of so-called alcohol-containing Shandy products are among the new line extensions for a number of brewers. So, was Chelsea simply a couple of decades ahead of its time, or should A-B not have tried to market it as a soft drink, which technically it was, in the first place?)

Twenty-Nine

After several years of imploring by the A-B marketing and PR brain trust, August Busch III finally agreed to serve as grand marshal of the 1980 Daytona 500, and it was clear from the outset that he'd much rather have had all his teeth pulled at once. However, he knew A-B had a big investment in NASCAR, so trooper that he was he swallowed hard and, with his usual intensity, fulfilled all of the various ceremonial duties he was called on to perform throughout the race weekend.

On race day, the instant the green flag fell and the race was underway he turned to me and asked if it was OK to head for home. I urged him to wait for twenty or twenty-five laps so that we could make a more polite exit. A plane was waiting for us at the Daytona airport, which is just a stone's throw from the racetrack. Our hosts, Bill France Sr. and Jr., arranged for us to have a police escort to the airport—two burly sheriff's deputies on Harley Hogs. Rather than use a paved road, however, they took a shortcut, ushering our town car across an open field, but one of them did not see a looming ditch and went ass over handlebars, hurting his pride far more than his body.

Ultimately we boarded the plane and flew first to Lakeland, as August and his wife, Ginny, had left their two young children there for the weekend at the home of his close friend, A-B distributor Bernie Little, and his wife, Jane. There were two conveyances waiting for us at the Lakeland airport—a Bell Jet Ranger and a Rolls Royce—and off we all went to fetch the kids. August assigned his executive assistant, Mike Carpenter, and me to ride in the backseat of the helicopter with him and Ginny up front. Lifting off, we realized that it was the novice Ginny, not August, at the controls, and Carpenter and I looked at each other with no small measure of alarm. After only six or seven minutes we began our descent; the destination was straight ahead, apparently on the other side of a row of Poplar trees that lined the shore of a lake. All Ginny had to do was thread a small opening in the tree line—seemingly similar to kicking a seventy-yard field goal in a football game with gale force headwinds. Somehow she did it, no problem, and as she set the contraption down the earth kicked up and a bevy of Little's resident peacocks scrambled away in fright.

"I need to change my underwear," Carpenter whispered as the flight ended. For the trip back to the airport we didn't wait for instructions; we jumped in the Rolls.

Thirty

I was home, half-asleep and sort of watching the late CBS network news on television one Sunday evening, when word came that Vladimir "Spider" Sabich, a star American downhill skier and jet-setter, was shot and killed by his girlfriend, Claudine Longet, a French-born actress-singer and ex-wife of crooner Andy Williams. Reportedly it happened during a domestic altercation in Aspen, Colorado.

The news jolted me awake. The previous weekend in Aspen the thirty-year-old Sabich competed in a Budweiser-sponsored ski race. He was captured there on film in a loving embrace with Longet by a photographer I'd hired to document the event. I guessed it might have been the last photo taken of the couple together in happier days. I hustled down to the office first thing the next morning, got into the files and, sure enough, there was the departed downhiller—resplendent in his Budweiser-labeled competition bib—strolling arm in arm with the demure Frenchwoman. I called a contact with United Press International (UPI), which was still a factor in journalism in those days, and in less than an hour the wire service transmitted the photo to virtually every newsroom in the free world. After that it appeared in literally hundreds of newspapers and magazines.

I notified some key Anheuser-Busch executives of the photo placement and received "atta boys" from the likes of Denny Long, Mike Roarty, and the Budweiser brand team.

One senior brewery executive was not so impressed, however. Fred Kuhlmann, the company's vice chairman, an older, straight-laced gentleman who managed the legal department and other administrative functions, scolded me for "inappropriately and distastefully exploiting a tragedy." I countered that I was simply trying to take advantage of a breaking news-related opportunity, that no one would know how it originated, and that the move had been greeted with approval by virtually everyone who counted in beer marketing. It seemed at the time that Kuhlmann, dubbed by one of my associates as "the corporate stick-in-the-mud," went out of his way to level the criticism; it was one of a number of dustups I would have over time with Fred, who I regarded as principled but sanctimonious and out of step with the company's new guard. He in turn likely viewed me as a troublesome hotshot who was tight with others in senior management—people with whom he vied for power and influence.

• • •

Fielding time-sensitive queries and interview requests from journalists became another ongoing source of friction between Kuhlmann and me. Fred was extremely cautious by nature and frequently out of the loop on day-to-day issues that could arise, prompting media interest. Often if I went to him for clearance of prepared statements or informal responses to reporters' questions he would indicate a need first to get up to speed on the matter and then to run it past Busch III, whether that was reasonably necessary or not. That could be a problem if the company's response was (A) important and (B) the reporter was on deadline. The other wrinkle: Fred was the client, and he had a major say in our relationship with A-B, not to mention control over a significant portion of our invoices. Nevertheless, we soldiered on and tried to handle each situation on a case-by-case basis.

• • •

One time, the always-proper Kuhlmann issued a corporate policy directive insisting that all employees who traveled on company business turn their accumulated frequent flyer miles over to the company. The edict was universally ignored, and so several months later Fred issued a second, more strident communiqué, this time emphasizing that employees who disregarded the mandate would face dire but unspecified consequences.

I saw the matter as a silly, heavy-handed attempt to deprive affected employees of a valued perk. Assisted by an inside accomplice, I drafted a widely circulated anonymous response memo that called on those suspecting others of ignoring the travel policy to snitch on their fellow employees. The new initiative would be known as Operation T.I.T., short for "Turn in a Traveler," and those who cooperated with the program would receive generous bounties in the form of free trips underwritten, of course, by the confiscated air miles of their coworkers.

Rank and file employees of course loved the phantom memo, and the policy was never enforced further.

• • •

My penchant for pranks and insulting humor was always looming just below the surface, especially if there was a chance to take a poke at something or someone pretentious or otherwise ridiculous. For example, as recalled by my esteemed former partner and friend, Jim Morice: "PR people tend to be pretty verbal and more than a little cynical. They don't tolerate fools unless they get paid for it, and they enjoy deflating one another's egos whenever possible, perhaps as compensation for taking such infinite care over those of their clients. One day in the era before e-mail, I was plodding though my work when a secretary came into my office, a large stack of memos under her arm and a harried expression on her face. Without a word she tossed the top sheet onto my desk and was out the door before I could ask her what was up. 'We are having Thanksgiving dinner with David Susskind,' the memo announced. It was addressed to everyone in the agency from the general manager of our

New York office. In case Susskind was before your time, he was a big deal on the network talk show circuit a while back, and I could almost hear the triumphal fanfare as my colleague let everyone know just how well connected he was. 'While I cannot spend the entire afternoon pitching David on behalf of our clients, contact me if you know of a prominent CEO who would be willing to discuss an interesting and hopefully controversial subject on the air.' Fat chance, I thought. CEOs welcome controversy almost as much as long-distance truck drivers enjoy stopping for a chat with the highway patrol.

"Within three minutes, another secretary entered my office, an equally large stack of paper under her arm. 'We are celebrating Easter with the Pope,' the memo she left behind said. 'It was from one of the senior officers of the company (yours truly) and like its predecessor went to everyone in the firm. 'While I cannot spend all afternoon advising Il Papa on what to say to the assembled multitude in Saint Peter's Square, please let me know if you have a client with strong opinions on liturgical reform, Vatican II or whether Cardinal Cody was getting it on with his cousin.'

"Within two minutes, a third secretary walked into my office carrying the now-familiar stack of paper. She was laughing. This memo was from yet another senior person in the firm, and once again went to every employee. 'We are having Thanksgiving with a turkey,' the note announced, 'and so is David Susskind.'"

• • •

Some attempts at humor backfired—big time—like the time someone sent me an item from my old hometown newspaper, the *Illinois State Journal-Register*. It turns out that a lifelong friend who'd gone on to become the top cardiothoracic surgeon in Central Illinois had filed suit against a state trooper. Seems like the good doctor was called to the hospital in the middle of the night because a patient had taken a turn for the worse and was on death's door. The good doctor got into his turbo Porsche and drove from his home on the south end of town to the hospital on the north side at speeds exceeding 100 mph. The trooper in question saw what was happening and gave chase, but could never catch up. The next night, the cop descended on my friend's residence and attempted to arrest him for speeding, leaving the scene and other infractions, and literally strong-armed his way into the house. Later I learned that my friend had earlier saved the life of the trooper's father with a triple bypass or some other procedure.

That was all the inspiration I needed to concoct a fictitious, seemingly humorous and harmless version of what happened, the fictional climax of which was that the trooper's dad came out of surgery transformed as his mother, and in this version my friend was being sued for malpractice.

Back then we had a state-of-the-art capability at F-H to send news releases and other communications to the news media electronically, similar to the regular wire services. So I turned my gag version of the story over to the woman in charge of this capability...asked her to set it up like a piece of wire service copy and to print it so that I could mail it to my friend...being careful not to hit the send button as it would end up in a dozen or so newsrooms and cause all sorts of consternation and confusion. Well, she blew the assignment. The item was indeed transmitted to all those newsrooms. Sensing a prank a couple of reporters called seeking more information on the matter. About then, John Graham found out about it and hit the ceiling. He called me out of a meeting at the brewery where I was going blissfully about my business unaware of the problem until that very moment and rightfully pinned the blame for the incident on me rather than the woman who was simply trying to do as she was asked. In time we all had a good laugh about it, but it took a while for the wounds—and my ego—to heal.

Thirty-One

Miller's lower-calorie Miller Lite beer and the ingenious ad campaign that ignited its sales was one of the major keys to the Milwaukee brewer's remarkable resurgence. For its commercials Miller memorably recruited a host of well-known former athletes and other notables to appear in various humorous settings engaging in a verbal tug of war over the product's attributes. "Tastes great," one spokes-jock would insist. "Less filling," countered another. The campaign ran for years with seemingly endless mutations.

Resorting to what amounted to a Hail Mary pass in hopes of derailing the Miller Lite beer express, the brain trust for Natural Light, Anheuser-Busch's unspectacular first foray into the lower calorie category, cooked up an ad campaign in which some of the original Miller Lite beer celebrities switched their allegiance to the A-B product. Naturally, they looked to us at Fleishman-Hillard to make a major publicity splash with the defections. The roster included some big names—baseball Hall of Famer Mickey Mantle; former heavyweight boxing champion the late Joe Frazier, up from Philadelphia in a limousine; Miami Dolphin linebacker Nick Buoniconti of "No Name Defense" fame; pitching great Jim "Catfish" Hunter; and former New York Knicks star Walt "Clyde" Frazier (no relation to Joe). The one constant in all of the commercials was comedian Norm Crosby, who had appeared in earlier Natural Light ads and so was already associated with the brand.

Since Crosby was a comic and fellow jokemeister and since Rodney Dangerfield appeared in some of the Miller Lite beer commercials, we decided to do a little ambush marketing and hold a press conference at Dangerfield's nightclub on New York's East Side. We arranged to have Crosby and all of the defecting ex-athletes on hand for the big announcement.

We booked Dangerfield's for a late morning news conference and the invitations were distributed. About a week before the event, our New York office's Wayne Charness and I visited the club to scope out the premises and plan the proceedings. (Charness later became the top PR and PA executive with Hasbro, Inc., retiring in early 2014 after an illustrious twenty-eight-year career there.) While there, Wayne got a phone call from Dangerfield's manager who'd somehow learned the purpose of our news conference. In view of Rodney's relationship with Miller, they could not allow his club to be used for an Anheuser-Busch ambush, the manager said. Charness put the caller on hold long enough to convey that news to me.

"Tell him OK, no problem, we'll make other arrangements," I instructed the flustered Charness. "What are you, freaking crazy?" he asked once the phone call ended. "This thing is happening a week from now. We're screwed."

"Trust me," I countered. "It's no big deal. We head back to the office. We book another venue—a better location, say, one of the Central Park South hotels—and we send out overnight Mailgrams to everyone we've invited. We say 'Due to circumstances beyond our control, we've had to relocate the Anheuser-Busch announcement originally scheduled for Dangerfield's to such-and-such a place.' The media will be curious to learn why. It will mean even better attendance and coverage. Guaranteed." That's what we did, and that's exactly what happened.

The night before the big announcement, Charness and I and a couple of the other publicists met Mickey Mantle for dinner at the Park Lane Hotel, just a few doors away from the Saint Moritz, which we'd booked in lieu of Dangerfield's. At the outset Mantle was sullen and subdued. It was almost as if he resented being there. But after his second vodka gimlet he relaxed, warmed up, and began telling hilarious stories about some of his playing days escapades with Billy Martin, Whitey Ford, and other Yankee stalwarts. Then at exactly 10:00 p.m. Mantle excused himself and said good night. He was seen a few minutes later boarding the hotel elevator with a stunning blonde.

The next morning's *Wall Street Journal* carried a front-page advance story on the campaign, engineered from Saint Louis by Dave Garino, a colleague and former *Journal* bureau chief. The news conference was an enormous success, with more than 125 reporters and TV crews covering. The celebrity defectors were introduced. The new ads were showcased. All made brief remarks, which were scripted to be humorous, and Norm Crosby was masterfully hilarious as emcee. Once the Natural Light sales results were known a few months later, however, it was apparent the publicity easily eclipsed the impact of the turnabout ad campaign.

Thirty-Two

Anheuser-Busch plunked down $11 million to sponsor the Summer Olympic Games to take place in Los Angeles some four years hence. The decision to do so was made in the wake of the 1980 Moscow games, which were boycotted by the United States and much of the rest of the free world to protest Russia's invasion of Afghanistan.

That was just a down payment on the brewery's Olympics commitment that ultimately would reach three or four times that level with advertising, entertainment, and other initiatives geared at leveraging the sponsorship. As such, the company's newly formed sports marketing group and its agencies received a mandate. "We need to be the first corporate sponsor out there with a unique, high-impact promotion that underscores that we're the corporate big dog when it comes to these games," Denny Long and Mike Roarty insisted. "We must get the drop on McDonalds…Coke…7-Eleven…and any of the others who'll no doubt be looking to make a big splash."

A short time later, Don Dixon, the company's first-ever sports marketing director, surfaced with a concept for a "unique, proprietary promotion with legs—something we can launch immediately and stay with until the Olympic torch burns atop the Los Angeles Coliseum." It called for the brewery to have former US Olympic gold medalists use the implements of their respective sports to create paintings with signed, limited edition prints to be sold to the general public—the proceeds benefiting the US Olympic cause. None of the so-called athlete-artists had prior artistic training, talent, or experience. But all would be famous and would represent a wide spectrum of Olympic sports. "PR has to carry the lion's share of the early load on this," Dixon emphasized. "What do you think?" he asked.

"It has some interesting possibilities," I said. "Who can we get to do the paintings? That's the key. Then we have to see how their work turns out. How much will you sell the prints for? Of course we'd need to document each painting session with photos and video. We might want to offer a behind-the-scenes exclusive to a handpicked reporter who'd attend some of the sessions, interview the athletes, and have a story ready to go when we take the wraps off the program. But if we really want this thing to be self-sustaining for three or four years, I'd like to suggest some extra wrinkles."

"Pray tell," Dixon said.

"For openers, we launch the promotion with a news conference in New York with all the gold medalists on hand. We announce that while the prints will be sold to the public, we'll arrange to have the originals sold at auction, and for extra credibility and topspin we get one of the silk stocking auction houses to handle that for us. Then after the auction we borrow the originals back from their new owners and take them on a national tour—shopping malls, ball parks, sports arenas, venues like that—and we bring in at least one of the athletes to hype each local showing, sign autographs, etc. We keep the originals moving and then have them on display for a grand finale of sorts at the Anheuser-Busch VIP hospitality center in LA during the '84 games. What do you think?"

"Awesome, but do you really think we can do all that?"

"It all depends on who does the paintings," I stressed again. Dixon then signed six outstanding former Olympians to participate: basketball great (and surprisingly surly) Bill Russell; ageless discus thrower Al Oerter; sprinter Wilma Rudolph; marathon runner Frank Shorter; swimmer John Naber; and Mike Eruzione, captain of the 1980 "Miracle on Ice" US hockey team and a hero of the gold-medal-winning performance at Lake Placid. (Oerter and Rudolph have since passed away.)

A kickoff news conference was held at the Waldorf-Astoria. The originals were on display and their creators were on hand for the announcement. The *Today* show gave the promotion ten minutes that morning, and *USA Today* had a front-page advance story. Through my friendship with the celebrated sports artist/illustrator Walt Spitzmiller, a Saint Louis native who'd moved east and hit it big, arrangements were made after the kickoff to display the works at a sports art gallery on West Fifty-Seventh Street; Bill Goff, the gallery owner, signed on to serve as curator and to coordinate the national tour.

The originals—large, bold, colorful abstract canvasses that represented no threat to the works or reputations of Pollack, Dali, or other postmodernists—would be sold at a luncheon back at the Waldorf, with Christie's agreeing to preside pro bono over the auction in light of the charitable aspect.

The big day finally arrived—May 13, 1981. Nearly five hundred luminaries from sports, entertainment, the media, and the business worlds paid one hundred dollars each to join August A. Busch III and other ranking Anheuser-Busch executives for a luncheon auction in the hotel's grand ballroom. About an hour beforehand, Gary Prindiville, the brewery's corporate security chief, approached me and said, "Too bad about the Pope getting shot, huh? That's not going to hurt us, is it?" Nerve-wracked as always before a big event, at first I thought he was kidding, only to learn a few minutes later that in fact John Paul II had been seriously wounded by a would-be assassin as he greeted religious pilgrims at the Vatican. It's too late to do anything about it now, I thought, certain it would impair news coverage of our event and just about everything else that wasn't of earth-shaking proportions that day and for several more.

Regardless, the auction went off flawlessly. The auctioneer, a glib six-foot, eight-inch Englishman, did a masterful job getting the crowd into the bidding. All told, the six works garnered $106,000, with the hockey captain's canvas selling for a remarkable $36,500. When asked to explain, he quipped, "There are hundreds of Picassos, but only one Eruzione."

Sparked by television ads, thousands of the signed and numbered prints were sold at $198.40 apiece. The national tour went forward, attracting excellent crowds. And the Budweiser Olympic Artwork program won a coveted Silver Anvil Award from the Public Relations Society of America, in those days the industry's Oscar. It was the first Silver Anvil ever won by Fleishman-Hillard in the hotly contested marketing category.

• • •

Perhaps because he'd never served in the military, August Busch III was enamored with men and women in uniform. For example, as construction of the Fairfield, California, brewery was nearing completion in the mid-1970s, he met and became impressed with General Tom Aldrich, the commandant at nearby Travis Air Force Base.

Aldrich, a major general, retired shortly thereafter, and August lost no time bringing him into the Anheuser-Busch fold as a vice president. The only problem was that he had few clear duties and seemed somewhat lost in the civilian business world. Based in California, however, he did serve on point as the brewery negotiated its 1984 Los Angeles Olympics sponsorship. The deal, with the Los Angeles Olympic Organizing Committee, did not give the company the naming rights to any of game's venues. However McDonald's, 7-Eleven, and some other big money players signed contracts giving them the naming rights of specific competition sites, about which "The General," as he was known, was heard to complain.

"At ten million dollars our deal was as big as or bigger than theirs. General, who negotiated it?" I asked rather snarkily.

Thirty-Three

On May 25, 1979, American Airlines flight 191, a DC-10 bound for Los Angeles, crashed just after takeoff from Chicago's O'Hare International Airport. All 271 souls onboard were killed. It was the third such catastrophe suffered by the jumbo jet over a several year period, but the first in US skies, and it resulted in the FAA temporarily grounding the aircraft.

In the wake of the tragedy and grounding, Harry Wilson received a call from the head of public relations for DC-10 manufacturer McDonnell Douglas (now Boeing) asking him and other agency personnel of his choosing to attend a meeting at the company's Saint Louis headquarters to discuss the crisis. Wilson asked me to tag along in view of my experience dealing with national media and what he termed "hot potatoes." With my time monopolized in recent years by Anheuser-Busch, I was delighted to accompany my old friend and agency mentor and to take a breather from my usual responsibilities.

We sat through a briefing on the technical, political, and business implications of the situation. "The DC-10 will be recertified for flight soon," we were told by Dick Davis, the company's public affairs chief. "The problem we fear is that the public won't want to fly on the aircraft. That will hurt American and the other carriers using the plane, to say nothing of how it impacts us. We can't let the airlines, our good customers, twist; we feel we must do something dramatic to restore the confidence of the flying public in the DC-10, which, by the way, is safe."

Davis and representatives of J. Walter Thompson, McDonnell Douglas's advertising agency, recommended television and print advertising extolling not only the virtues of the DC-10, but stressing that for decades the company produced safe, superior commercial and military aircraft and was the lead original contractor for the US space program, beginning with the very beginning—the halcyon Mercury and Gemini project eras.

"If Old Man Mac (company founder James S. McDonnell) were not on his death bed as we speak, we couldn't even begin to consider this move. He would never hear of it," Davis said. Then he asked Wilson and me what we thought of the idea. When it was my turn to weigh in, I applauded the plan wholeheartedly and offered additional recommendations which, I was confident, could make the campaign even more effective. I enthusiastically endorsed the ad agency's proposed use of Charles "Pete" Conrad as the spokesperson in the commercials. A former test pilot, the third person to walk on the Moon, and at that point a McDonnell Douglas vice president, Pete was perfect for the role. He was a natural performer and the poster boy for the swashbuckling first generation of the astronaut corps lionized in literature by Tom Wolfe and by Hollywood in the movie version of *The Right Stuff.*

I recommended taking the wraps off the campaign plans and previewing the TV spots at a news conference in New York with the company represented by Conrad, CEO Sanford McDonnell (the founder's nephew), and a bevy of technical experts.

I encouraged the company to produce a definitive position paper on the situation and to offer it free via the ads to the public and to key constituencies—airline executives, politicians, travel agents, and others.

Also, I suggested technical briefings in Washington, DC, for members of Congress, transportation safety officials, key trade associations, and ranking executives of airlines that use DC-10 equipment.

Finally, I proposed having Conrad visit other key markets—hometowns of airlines and relevant airline hub cities, for example, to do media interviews on the campaign and the DC-10.

The ads were produced and the launch announcement was set for the New York Hilton Hotel in Midtown Manhattan. A panel of key

McDonnell Douglas executives would hold forth as proposed—headlined by "Sandy" McDonnell and Pete Conrad. The commercials were shown, prepared remarks were delivered, and all went as planned until the question-answer session began. Then *ABC News* Science Editor Jules Bergman and his *New York Times* counterpart, Richard Witkin (who also was Bergman's brother-in-law), took turns asking tough technical questions about the Chicago crash and two earlier ones in Europe until they were all but skewering the panel. Flustered, Sandy McDonnell got up and stalked indignantly out of the room, followed by camera crews and reporters, thus ruining an otherwise successful press function. Ironically and lamentably, McDonnell's in-house handlers opted not to put their boss through agency-recommended rehearsals intended to guard against the disastrous incident that occurred.

A first wave of the ads ran and was well received, but within a few weeks McDonnell pulled the plug on the commercials and scuttled the rest of the initiative. The public remained wary of the DC-10, and McDonnell Douglas never took another order for the passenger-carrying version of the $40 million flying behemoths.

"The client's always right; only God can save these poor bastards from themselves," I commiserated with Harry Wilson.

(Our DC-10 work later resulted in F-H receiving an opportunity to handle crisis communications in the wake of the disastrous 1980 MGM Grand Hotel fire in Las Vegas that claimed the lives of eighty-four people.)

Thirty-Four

Budweiser sales languished for a time in the wake of the epic, one hundred-day strike until D'Arcy, then the agency of record for the brand, came under do or die pressure with a catchy new ad campaign themed "This Bud's for You." The commercials, strikingly similar to Miller's High Life ads, were a salute to American workers and featured real people at work rather than actors or models commonly used in adult beverage advertising.

("This Bud's for You" rescued the brand from a tailspin, brought on in part by a disastrous, short-lived campaign themed "Welcome Home." It was the conceptual brainchild of Russell Ackoff, a doctrinaire Wharton School management professor who had exceptional influence with Busch III and, as history has shown, was anything but infallible when it came to the marketing realm. Forced upon D'Arcy, the brewery's lead agency at the time, "Welcome Home" depicted consumers enjoying the product in their homes, backyards, and other "off-premise" settings. Fair enough, but it ignored the role of away-from-home consumption—in more lively settings such as bars, restaurants, hotels, sporting events, and the like, prompting a near mutiny by the brewery's more than nine hundred distributors, back then, and legions of "on-premise" retailers. "Welcome Home" was not welcome anywhere, or so it seemed. And, curiously enough, almost no one remembers it today.)

• • •

With "This Bud's for You" at full gallop and Budweiser sales responding nicely, I got a call from one of the brewery's attack dogs, a staff lawyer responsible for policing the company's intellectual property—copyrights, trademarks, and the like. He said a mom and pop florist shop in Houston, Texas, was using the new ad slogan, a registered service mark, to promote the sale of roses. The brewery was preparing to seek an injunction to halt to the practice. The flower shop was a small business owned and operated by a middle-aged woman. The attorney wanted me to prepare a news release on the pending action.

Having had some previous trademark and licensing-related experience and fully appreciating the importance of such enforcement, I had some unexpected advice for the attorney. "Don't do it," I urged. "There's a fine line between infringement and flattery. When this goes public, you'll make an instant martyr out of this woman. Anheuser-Busch will appear unreasonably heavy handed—anti-woman and anti–small business. It'll be David versus Goliath. And it will be playing out in the Lone Star State, the most hotly contested beer market in the country. It has lose-lose written all over it."

"Sorry, no can do," the lawyer said, and off he went to seek the injunction.

I alerted our Texas affiliate of the looming flap, and together we worked on a statement for use when the press got wind of the situation. "All we can do is defend the practice of protecting our intellectual property no matter what; we'll have to assert that the company has nothing against small business in general or this woman in particular, but that will be of limited help with a bunch of self-righteous reporters nipping at our heels," I predicted.

Sure enough, in short order the lady florist from Houston who was just trying to sell a few flowers became an overnight *cause celeb.* She and her plight were documented sympathetically in *People* magazine; the wire services and broadcast networks picked it up from there. The issue remained front and center for a few days until her lawyer and attorneys for the company reached a quiet settlement.

All I could do was shake my head and ironically, in the eyes of some brewery executives who did not know better, take the bullet for a bad PR move.

Thirty-Five

With a new brewery about to open in Fairfield in Northern California, its tenth nationwide, Anheuser-Busch assumed sponsorship of a professional golf tournament previously known as the Kaiser Open, Kaiser Industries having opted to discontinue its involvement. The seventy-two-hole PGA Tour event was played at Silverado, the landmark resort and spa in the heart of the Napa wine country, not far from Fairfield.

Now it would be called the Anheuser-Busch Golf Classic, chaired by Orion Burkhardt, a golf fanatic and former marketing vice president who'd moved on to serve as the brewery's industry and government affairs honcho. Burkhardt asked me to serve on the tournament's executive committee, overseeing the press room, credentialing, and media relations. I was delighted to oblige.

The tournament was a big deal with locals who did not want to see it leave the area or collapse following Kaiser's decision to bail. It was also a big hit with the brewery's distributors, many of whom were anxious to play in the charity-benefitting pro-am tournament preceding championship play. For them it was a blast—a five-day party in one of the most magnificent settings imaginable, and a chance to rub shoulders with professional golf's elite. (Miller Barber, a colorful albeit eccentric Southerner, won the inaugural A-B Classic.)

For year two, Burkhardt pulled out all stops. He arranged for Ed McMahon to emcee the proceedings and recruited baseball greats Stan Musial, Joe Garagiola, and Roger Maris to play in the Wednesday pro-am along with matinee idol Clint Eastwood and Nathaniel Crosby, Bing's son and a one-time US amateur champion. Musial and Garagiola were teammates on the 1946 Saint Louis Cardinals World Series championship team. Musial was one of the best to ever play the game and the consensus greatest Cardinal of all time. Garagiola, a journeyman catcher, went on to gain national fame as a witty baseball announcer, quiz show host, and coanchor of the *Today* show. Maris, of course, broke Babe Ruth's long-standing single season record, hitting sixty-one homers in 1961 as a New York Yankee. Traded to Gussie Busch's Cardinals, he received a beer distributorship in Gainesville, Florida, for agreeing to play in Saint Louis for several more seasons. With Maris in right field, the Cardinals won pennants in 1967 and '68. However, after his experiences with the New York sports writers, many of whom resented his home-run achievement, the unassuming Maris had a less than amicable relationship with the press.

Venerable Bay Area sports columnist Art Spander asked me to invite Musial, Garagiola, and Maris to stop by the press room after their rounds. "Just see if they'll shoot the breeze with us for a while, since the pro-am typically doesn't provide much to write about," Spander suggested. All three agreed, and there were a dozen or so writers on hand when they arrived. We arranged to have drinks served, and when the session ended nearly three hours later, the writers had heard more baseball war stories—funny and otherwise—than they could possibly digest, much less write about. It was a rare and magical afternoon.

(Tom Watson won the Anheuser-Busch Golf Classic that year. Roger Maris died of cancer in 1985 at the age of fifty-one. Musial and Garagiola eventually would have a falling out over a business partnership.)

• • •

The following year Burkhardt called and said, "We want to move the tournament over to the other coast—to our course at Kingsmill in Virginia. With the move the Tour will give us a better date for the event, and we'll be on network television for the first time. So if you're the PR man you're cracked up to be, figure out how we can do it without alienating half of Northern California," he added facetiously.

Several days later, Burkhardt received a letter from AmFac, the Honolulu-based owner of Silverado, indicating that for various reasons they did not intend to renew as the host venue of the tournament. "How's that for taking care of a touchy issue?" I asked Orion, tongue-in-cheek. Barely able to disguise our euphoria, we flew to Napa and released the contents of the AmFac letter to the local news media, stressing that the company regretted the decision, appreciated the support of Northern Californians, and was evaluating its future location options.

After a few weeks, to no one's surprise, flanked by defending champion Ben Crenshaw and Kingsmill resident and pro tour member Curtis Strange, Burkhardt announced that future installments of the tournament would be played in Williamsburg. After the news conference Burkhardt and I met with Strange, who expressed regret about a nasty exchange he'd just had with a lady heckler in the gallery at Arnold Palmer's Bay Hill Invitational tournament in Florida. The incident was witnessed by many and was widely reported in the press. Afterward, Strange apologized in writing to the woman and to Mr. Palmer. "I've learned my lesson; from now on I'm going to be Joe Jovial out there on tour," he said. "You can't be what you aren't, so don't even try," I counseled Strange. "You're by nature too competitive and intense to do that. Be yourself. Stay focused—just don't piss anybody off."

Soon Strange won his first PGA Tour championship, the Houston Open. He went on from there to win seventeen times on the Tour, including back-to-back US Opens, and was the first player ever to earn $1 million in purse money in a single season. He captained the losing 2002 US Ryder Cup team and has worked for several years as a television golf analyst in addition to competing on the PGA's Champions Tour, formerly known as the Senior Tour.

• • •

It was an especially touchy time for Anheuser-Busch and, indeed, other companies that sponsored sports events. In the so-called name of journalistic purity, led by the wire services, most major news organizations refused to call tournaments and other sports events by their sponsored names, claiming at the time that it was too commercial. The Anheuser-Busch Golf Classic was a victim of that policy as were most other golf and tennis tournaments, auto races, and a host of other sporting events. This put considerable pressure not only on the corporate executives who wrote the checks but also those of us in the PR realm. "Why are we spending all those millions of dollars if we can't get exposure and credit for it via the news coverage?" was the typical complaint.

Tired of all the justified bitching and moaning, I prevailed on Burkhardt to accompany me to New York to meet with key decision makers at the wire services and other news organizations, chief among them being Associated Press sports editor Wick Temple, who gave us a good hearing. We based our case on several considerations, reporting accuracy being the first, and we offered a not-so-veiled threat that if the media would not see the light, corporate sports sponsorships would go the way of the buggy whip. We also lobbied sanctioning groups like the PGA Tour to bring pressure to bear on the media organizations.

Eventually the practice ended. The groundwork we and others laid, together with the emergence of less-picky ESPN, contributed to the about-face and today's much more liberal media practices as they relate to commercially sponsored sports.

Thirty-Six

"I hate this fucking game, but I have all these matching outfits." The quipster was comedy legend Bob Hope, and the source of his feigned irritation was golf. His audience: yours truly. The location: just off stage at Saint Louis's Millennium Hotel, where there was a gala dinner underway celebrating the grand opening and dedication of the Saint Louis Soccer Park, a European-style complex in the suburbs.

I'd worked with Hope a number of times. A couple of years earlier he played in Lee Elder's charity tournament at Kingsmill, outside Williamsburg, Virginia. Elder was a Michelob-sponsored fixture on the PGA Tour, and in 1975 became the first African-American to play in the Masters. He and his wife, Rose, established a charitable foundation to introduce golf to inner-city youngsters. Some funding for the program came from his annual tournament, which attracted celebrities from sports, politics, entertainment, and business. Hope was one of a galaxy of notables at Kingsmill that year, including former President Gerald Ford; US House Speaker "Tip" O'Neill; Teamsters President Frank Fitzsimmons, and various current and former athletes, but Hope was the big draw, and I staffed the event, coordinating media coverage and working with the luminaries.

(Another time I worked with Hope as he entertained at an Anheuser-Busch sales convention in San Francisco. Even though he was in his eighties, the indefatigable showman sang, danced, and told jokes for more than two hours for a private audience of more than one thousand beer distributors and company employees.)

The Soccer Park was a lifelong dream of Denny Long, a godfather of the sport in Saint Louis, which had spawned many outstanding amateur, collegiate, and professional stars—mainly Catholics of Italian, German, and Irish descent. Bygones being bygones, Mike Roarty prevailed on his good friend Howard Cosell to serve as the evening's main speaker. By sheer coincidence, Hope was in Saint Louis to do his one-man show at the Fox Theater. Roarty, quite a showman in his own right, imposed on Hope to make a surprise cameo appearance at the event, promising he could be back at the Fox in time for his show. To make sure he kept his word, Roarty asked me to meet Hope's limousine when it arrived at the hotel, ushering him to a location just off stage. Serving as emcee of the function, Roarty got a bit long-winded in his introduction. Hope got antsy and began swinging an imaginary golf club. "Hurry up, Mike, I've got a show to do," Hope implored. Suddenly he stopped swinging, looked straight at me, and dropped his F-bomb. Moments later he was onstage basking in a standing ovation from a surprised and adoring crowd.

As time has passed, I've enjoyed telling others about the time the great Bob Hope told me a private joke. "It may not have been his A-material, but it was golf related and uncharacteristically raunchy," I'd add, strictly for contextual clarity.

Thirty-Seven

One afternoon a secretary popped into my office with a verbatim transcript of that morning's nationally syndicated *The Phil Donohue Show*. The broadcast featured representatives of MADD, the Mothers Against Drunk Driving organization, who'd lobbied effectively for stiffer penalties for those convicted of drunk driving and the lowering of the legal definition of intoxication in many states.

As Donohue listened to his guests' tales of tragic losses at the hands of drunk drivers, he interrupted the discussion, stood up, threw his arms in the air, and with great theatrics asserted, "Those people at Schlitz and Budweiser are butchers, murderers. We're going to have their presidents on the show and make them tell us why they're letting this happen." During the tirade he singled out no other brewers or other producers of alcoholic beverages, to say nothing about the disease of alcoholism.

Later that morning, I got a call from one of Donohue's producers who said her boss wanted to invite August Busch III to appear on a future program. "There's not a snowball's chance of that happening," I said. "Your guy called him a butcher and a killer this morning, which he's not. In fact no other brewer or distiller is doing nearly as much to foster responsible consumption of its products. I'd be crazy to advise him to go on your show to be torn apart by the host, whose sole objective is sensational television; he has no interest in anything close to a balanced segment or the public interest."

"Phil's not going to like hearing this," the producer said.

"Not my problem," I said, and the phone call ended.

A little later, my phone rang again. "This is Phil Donohue," the voice on the other end said. (There was no doubt that's who it was.) "What's this you're claiming that I called Mr. Busch some bad names? I did no such thing. We want to have him on the show to talk about what the company and the industry are doing to fight drunk driving and related problems." Donohue went on and on in that vein until finally, I asked, "Are you finished?" Then I read Donohue's exact words from the transcript and repeated for his benefit the reason for my declining to take the invitation to Mr. Busch.

"You know we're going to talk about your refusal to cooperate on our next show, don't you?" Donohue threatened.

"Please do, and when Mr. Busch hears about it he'll probably give me a gold star for doing my job," I said. "When you do that be sure to replay the tape of today's on-air diatribe. Your viewers will appreciate it, especially the thoughtful ones."

Of course the threatened follow-up segment never happened, and no doubt Busch III was never aware of any of it.

Thirty-Eight

Try as it might, Anheuser-Busch could not recapture its hold on the Chicago market after the 1976 strike, and August Busch III was furious. "Old Style," flagship of the G. Heileman Brewing Company, along with the Miller brands, commanded the lion's share of the Windy City's beer business, having wrested it away from Budweiser and other A-B products.

The company poured millions of extra dollars into the market to no avail. Along with representatives of both of its advertising agencies I was called to a meeting to discuss the dilemma, with Busch III presiding. A senior account executive with D'Arcy, the Budweiser agency, took the floor and suggested that if the company really wanted to make inroads in the market it should consider doing a product endorsement deal with Chicago Cubs announcer Harry Caray—he of the trademark Coke bottle glasses and the "Holy cow!" exclamation whenever a noteworthy play happened.

As those words were uttered the room fell deathly silent; I could have sworn I heard a chorus of gulps. A native Saint Louisan, Caray was the voice of the Cardinals for twenty-five years and a gin rummy playing pal of old Gussie Busch. But he was terminated abruptly in 1969. No official explanation was given for the dismissal; the rumor mill had it that while he was hospitalized recuperating from injuries sustained after a serious traffic mishap, Caray became involved with Susan Busch, the first (and former) wife of August III.

Then, after a year of broadcasting Oakland Athletics games, followed by several seasons in Chicago with the White Sox, the colorful Caray was lured to the north side of town—to Wrigley Field—where he held forth for decades with the Cubs, becoming an institution. Often seen after games making the rounds of Chicago's more popular nightclubs and restaurants, Caray became known as "The Mayor of Rush Street."

"What'll it take?" Busch III asked, the silence still palpable. "I'll need a day or two to find out, August," the ad man said.

Just like that, Harry Caray was under contract to do the Cubs games with Budweiser as his principal sponsor. We staged a news conference to announce the relationship and to preview commercials, produced exclusively for the Chicago market, in which the indomitable Caray proclaimed, "I'm a Cubs Fan and a Bud Man." Even though he did not attend the news conference, August Busch III demonstrated once again he would stop at nothing to sell his beer and regain what he believed was rightfully his.

Thirty-Nine

"It must drive you nuts to be paying your shortstop more than the fellow who's responsible for building your breweries," I ventured. August Busch III was at the wheel of the rented Buick—my rented Buick. We had just come from ceremonies marking the tripling of the production capacity of the company's Van Nuys, California, brewery. After the event, I was waylaid by the CEO, who wanted a ride back to our hotel, and of course Busch insisted on driving. As we barreled along Interstate 405, the San Diego Freeway, the discussion turned to the company's ownership of the Saint Louis Cardinals. Busch said nothing in response to my question. He didn't need to—his heavy right foot and white knuckles on the steering wheel betrayed his reaction, to say nothing of the veins popping out of his neck and the shade of crimson his face had turned. The shortstop, Garry Templeton, was making $600,000 that season; the company's construction and engineering vice president probably a third to a half of that.

With the onset of free agency, the economics of baseball changed radically. That left the Cardinals technically unprofitable, which was unacceptable to Busch III, who believed all of the company's business units should be self-supporting. When Saint Louis's new riverfront stadium was built a decade or so earlier, Anheuser-Busch civic-mindedly agreed to forego income from concessions and parking at the facility. The brewery and a dozen other Saint Louis corporations financed the construction and thus were shareholders in a semipublic, semiprivate stadium authority known as Civic Center, Inc. Anheuser-Busch was the largest investor with nearly a 25 percent stake in the venture. In return, the facility was named Busch Memorial Stadium.

So in 1981, Busch III approached Civic Center seeking to renegotiate the arrangement to enable the brewery to realize added revenues, thus offsetting its dramatically increasing player salary costs. He was summarily rejected. Smarting, he attempted a hostile takeover of Civic Center, tendering a cash offer for other outstanding shares. At that point, the Cardinals and the stadium were in play. Marvin Davis, a Denver oil tycoon, surfaced offering more for the shares than the initial Anheuser-Busch bid. It was thought at the time that Davis sought to acquire the team in order to move it to the Mile High City. Then Anthony Novelly, a publicity shy local oilman, made an even sweeter bid; his true interest was believed to be Civic Center's formidable real estate holdings. The concern was that if Novelly was successful he might turn around and sell the ball club to out of town interests. Busch didn't want to be a party to that. I was in the room and could hear the speakerphone conversation when Busch III spoke with Novelly. He sounded momentarily as if he might be ready to capitulate. "You can have the stadium and the rest of the property, but it's a package deal—you have to take the Cardinals too, and you have to guarantee that the team stays put," he told the suitor, whose interest in the deal pretty much evaporated then and there.

Finally, notwithstanding their earlier difficulties, August prevailed on his father to put the touch on several of his old cronies to tender their Civic Center shares on the heels of a sweetened Anheuser-Busch offer. In the end, the company got more than 51 percent of the stock and with it the stadium, the adjacent parking garages, a riverfront hotel, and other property all for approximately $53 million. Anheuser-Busch got the control and the added revenues it sought. As the saga played out, our communications emphasized the benefits to the competitiveness of the ball club and the overall community.

Forty

Emboldened by successful deals with several prominent Fortune 500 companies, including Coca-Cola and Kentucky Fried Chicken, the Reverend Jesse Jackson trained his sights on Anheuser-Busch.

A renowned shakedown artist, Jackson announced his goal was to reach a formal covenant by which the brewery would promise to have a specified number of minority-owned distributorships and various other business and financial initiatives that supposedly benefited the African-American community. However, he underestimated the company's record—the breadth and scope of its minority programs and the alliances it had forged—with both the Black and Hispanic communities. He also underestimated August A. Busch III, whose resolve precluded any possibility of an accord and all but guaranteed an outcome other than what Jackson had in mind.

Jackson called for black consumers to boycott Anheuser-Busch products as he visited brewery sites around the country. At each stop, of course with great dramatic flair for the benefit of the local news media, he popped open cans of the company's products, poured the liquid down a drain, and declared "Bud is a Dud."

But Fleishman-Hillard had Anheuser-Busch ready to rumble. Wherever Jackson appeared, the brewery's ranking black executive, Wayman Smith—an attorney and former Saint Louis alderman with exceptional national contacts and polemic skills—shadowed the reverend. In a style reminiscent of an old political truth squad, Smith conducted press briefings following each Jackson performance, handing out information on the company's comprehensive minority programs, which were becoming more impressive with each passing day. Realizing he could not bring Anheuser-Busch to heel, his perspective perhaps influenced by powerful Washington attorney Edward Bennett Williams, Jackson abandoned his crusade. Leaving nothing to chance, we orchestrated the public portion of the counterattack, making sure Jackson had all he could handle and that Wayman Smith was exactly where he needed to be at all times.

Years later Jackson's son, Yusef, was granted an Anheuser-Busch distributorship in the Chicago market. By then I was no longer involved with the brewery, but after all they'd been through, the decision to make young Jackson a wholesaler was certainly a curious turn of events.

Out of the frying pan...

Forty-One

One especially thorny issue that dogged Anheuser-Busch for years was a gun control rumor. It took various forms, but essentially we would get a call or a letter from a consumer who'd heard, always through the grapevine, that the Busch family and/or Anheuser-Busch was providing major financial support for some unspecified clandestine campaign to bring about national gun control legislation. Pro-gun interests who knew of the rumor and gave it credence were urging like-minded consumers to boycott Anheuser-Busch products. It was a complete fabrication, yet every time we thought we'd quashed the damn thing it would pop up somewhere else. When we asked inquiring individuals where they had heard the report, or from whom, it was usually from some unspecified person they'd encountered in a bar or package store but whose name they did not know or could not recall.

Certain it was spawned by a competitor, and determined to contain it, we'd send the respondent a package of information we'd developed that would convince any reasonable person that there was absolutely no truth to the rumor. It included reprints of stories from various publications (*Guns & Ammo, Field & Stream,* etc.) accurately portraying members of the Busch family as avid sportsmen who hunted, owned extensive gun collections, maintained hunting lodges, were longtime NRA and Ducks Unlimited members, etc. The package even included a story we'd placed in *Fortune* magazine about August Busch III's trapshooting prowess.

The rumor finally petered out but not until we offered a significant cash reward to anyone who could come forward with the verifiable name and whereabouts of anyone spreading the falsehood. No one ever qualified for the reward, but that seemed to take care of the problem once and for all.

• • •

Besides competition-caused rumors that were 100 percent false and that preyed on consumers' gullibility, we had to deal with leaks—the appearance of sensitive inside information or trade secrets in the news media. Fortunately we did not have to deal with such annoyances all that often, but when they did happen they were invariably followed by senior management explosions and, naturally, those of us on the PR front lines got the lion's share of the collateral shrapnel, figuratively speaking.

There was one especially troublesome situation involving a columnist for the local *Business Journal.* It seemed like every week or two he came up with a new scoop about something the brewery was planning but not yet ready to announce or introduce on either the product or marketing front, or in some cases did not want made public. Not only did he do so repeatedly, but with uncanny accuracy. Clearly he had an inside source either within the company or one of its key vendors. We never could determine who the culprit was, much less what the source's motivation might have been. As the designated firewall between the company and the media of course we were prime suspects in leakgate, but that made no sense given our responsibilities and consequent vulnerability. Busch III and other top executives got angrier and more paranoid with each disclosure.

Eventually the leaks stopped. Thankfully. That took the pressure off of us and prevented what might have been regrettable and indefensible behavior by some A-B loyalists who offered to personally take care of the problem.

Forty-Two

With the possible exceptions of tournament bridge or championship lawn billiards, few sports are more obscure than unlimited hydroplane racing, yet boat owner Bernie Little thought he should be *Sports Illustrated*'s "Sportsman of the Year" every year. And Bernie was upset.

The flamboyant Lakeland, Florida, beer distributor's Miss Budweiser perennially dominated the big boat circuit, and he wanted his due. Little also was one of Busch III's closest personal friends; he thought nothing of using that relationship to get what he wanted from the company whenever he wanted it, often with the heaviest hand he could wield. Rank and file brewery marketing people dreaded hearing from Little. They believed his racing team was disproportionately well funded in light of the small following the sport commanded. Also, Little was not a team player—he insisted on having all of his own resources, including a publicist, paid for of course by the brewery. There was nothing anyone could do about it; God help 'em if they tried.

Unlimited hydroplanes are the behemoths of boat racing. Powered by jet aircraft engines, they easily exceed 150 miles an hour and have a nasty tendency to go airborne, literally, often meaning disaster—especially for the driver.

I'd had a number of dealings with Little over time, always giving him a wide berth. However, one day I received a call from the publicist for the Miss Budweiser, whose professional credentials were impeccable—she was a tall, leggy blonde with store-bought physical assets and a deep Florida tan. "Bernie is going to fire me if I don't get a story in *Sports*

Illustrated," she said. "We hired a freelance writer out of Miami who's worked for the magazine before. He wrote something, but the editors keep sending it back saying it needs work. Can you help?"

I asked to see the freelancer's work. Then I ran the question by Wayne Charness in Fleishman-Hillard's New York office. Wayne was one of the Big Apple's most accomplished publicists. We concurred that the freelancer's piece would never qualify for publication in *Sports Illustrated.* "It's a pure puff piece on Little. It might be fine for the Air Florida in-flight magazine if there is such a thing, but it's definitely not *SI*-worthy," he said." However, we concluded there might be a story angle that *Sports Illustrated* would consider after all, but only if Little and his PR gal would let us go back to square one, jettisoning the freelance piece, and only if they understood that there were no guarantees.

"The real story here is the boat's driver, not Bernie Little," I told her, being sure to explain slowly enough so that she could understand and take the message back to her hell-bent boss. The driver, Dean Chenoweth, had survived several spectacular crashes and had gone on to win a number of races; he was about to win another Thunderboat series championship. He was the third Miss Budweiser pilot to drive for Little in five or six years, some of the others having perished in crashes, or simply had enough. "Of course you understand that if *Sports Illustrated* does agree to do a story, Bernie will be included; they'll have to give him his propers," I explained. "He also needs to know there'll be questions about the sport's extraordinary danger factor."

She got back to me to say that Little understood the implications, and he'd like to move forward. Charness pitched the idea, and *Sports Illustrated* agreed to do a full-blown feature on the heroics of the indomitable Chenoweth. Coles Phinizy, a grizzled veteran *SI* staff writer, was assigned to do the piece. He spent the better part of two weeks in Florida, lounging on Little's yacht, drinking his booze, eavesdropping on the principals and, oh yes, watching a couple of boat races.

The story appeared under the headline "Crash and Carry On," and it was a dandy. Several photos of an airborne Miss Budweiser and a jaunty, devil-may-care Chenoweth accompanied it. Bernie Little got his due as the sport's winningest team owner; Phinizy observed that a souvenir brochure for the boat depicted Little in photos with every VIP imaginable "with the possible exception of Santa Claus and the Pope," noting too that Little said he could not remember the names of all the men who had perished driving for him or how many there were.

In Saint Louis, the Budweiser brand team applauded the article. "We finally got some good exposure in return for the millions we've spent on a sport almost no one follows," one of them told me appreciatively and very much off the record.

Alas, I never heard a word from Bernie Little or his publicity gal about the article.

Six months later, Dean Chenoweth, who'd been given the Anheuser-Busch Tallahassee beer distributorship for his daring feats, was killed in a crash while driving the Miss Budweiser in Washington State.

(Bernie Little died of natural causes in 2003 at the age of seventy-eight. In 2004 Budweiser dropped out of unlimited hydroplane racing.)

Forty-Three

Hollywood icon (the late) Paul Newman was a renowned beer drinker. His original brand of choice was Coors. After starring in the motion picture *Winning* in the late 1960s, Newman took up automobile racing, and he was good at it. He drove souped-up sports cars on road racing courses for a team backed by the Nissan factory and owned by fellow Connecticut resident, Bob Sharp. Budweiser was the Sharp team's other major backer, so Newman switched to Bud.

Newman won several Sports Car Club of America (SCCA) championships driving for Sharp Racing. One weekend he was in Saint Louis to compete at Mid-America Raceway, a long-gone track about thirty miles west of the city. I'd just returned home from a business trip and got a call from Bob Thomas, my old West Coast affiliate who also represented Nissan; he was one of few publicists who had a good relationship with the prickly Newman. Thomas and Fleishman-Hillard combined at one point to capitalize on that relationship, convincing *People* magazine to do a cover story on Newman as an accomplished racecar driver rather than a screen idol. With Newman in town to race, Thomas asked, "Would you and Kathy be available this evening to have dinner with Paul Newman, me, and a couple of other people? We're meeting at eight o'clock at Anthony's Restaurant downtown." We scrambled around, got a babysitter for the kids, and set out for the posh five-star restaurant.

It was an awkward evening. Newman was petulant and self-absorbed. We had little in common with the star but tried to act blasé—so as not to seem intrusive or to convey the impression that we were awed by his celebrity. The only time Newman seemed to enjoy himself and open up was when he recalled a recent experience driving offshore cigarette racing boats at breakneck speeds off Baja in the Gulf of California while high on beer and marijuana.

He did however invite us to visit the racetrack and attend his ritual barbecue in the paddock area the following afternoon. "What can I bring?" Kathy asked.

"Not a thing," Newman said.

"I have this wonderful recipe for barbecued shrimp," she said. "It makes for a perfect appetizer."

"I'm not real keen on shrimp," he countered.

Undeterred, the next day Kathy bought twenty-five or thirty pounds of the best jumbo shrimp she could find, soaked them in her special marinade, and brought them to the cookout where they were grilled and quickly devoured.

"Damn good shrimp," Newman admitted, helping himself to seconds and thirds as they emerged from the grill.

Kathy had the recipe printed under the heading "Kathy Finnigan's World Famous Barbecued Shrimp a.k.a. Paul Newman's Revenge." I sent the first copy to *Post-Dispatch* gossip columnist Jerry Berger. He was delighted to have an honest-to-goodness Paul Newman item for his column.

(Not long after, Newman's son, Scott, died, reportedly of a drug overdose. His father established a foundation in his memory to discourage drug abuse. It's not known, but reasonably assumed, that he no longer reveled in his beer and marijuana-powered exploits.)

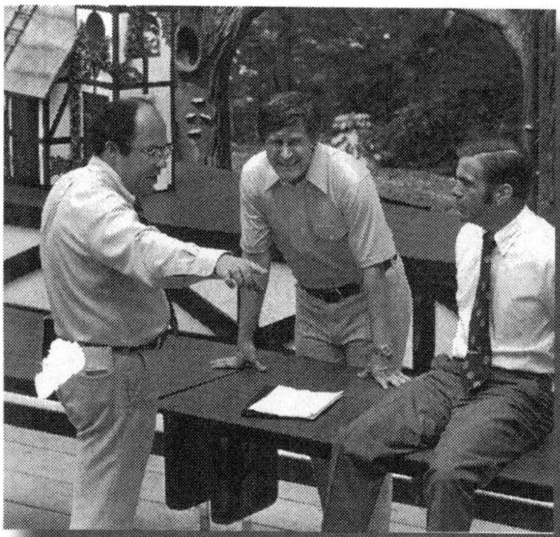

The author, left, briefs Dennis Long, center, and August A. Busch III on plans for the grand opening of Busch Gardens, Williamsburg, VA

Graveside at the American Cemetery, Omaha Beach

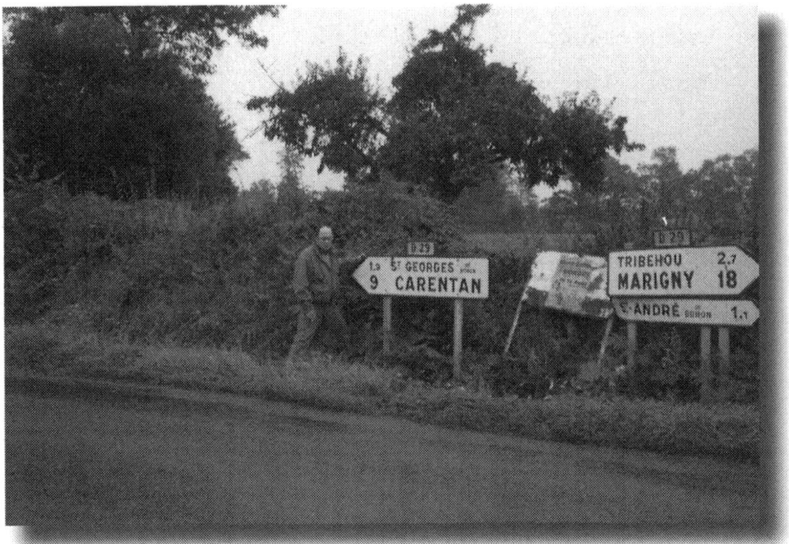

In the Normandy hedgerows near where the author's father died in combat on July 8, 1944

Fleishman-Hillard Chairman John Graham clowns with the author, seated, at an agency planning meeting in Newport Beach, CA

With Anheuser-Busch and other clients clamoring to get into auto racing, I saw an opportunity to establish a motor sports group at F-H. Sponsoring companies were spending millions to participate, and we convinced them that without proper PR support they were not getting their money's worth. For obvious reasons the Paul Newman/Bob Sharp venture did not need our help, they were covered by Nissan, but other Anheuser-Busch sponsorships did, as did Emerson Electric, Valvoline Oil, and Beatrice Foods, which made a huge commitment to the Carl Haas team and driver Mario Andretti and which ultimately cost Beatrice CEO James Dutt his job. We recruited a group of experienced communicators—former journalists primarily, who knew the ins and outs of the sport as well as the drivers, team owners, and media—and embedded them with assigned race teams. F-H Motor Sports was a business success for a number of years, with highlights including a 1986 Indianapolis 500 win for Budweiser-sponsored Bobby Rahal and Al Unser Junior's 1992 Indy championship for Valvoline.

Forty-Four

In 1980, former movie and television star, FDR Democrat turned conservative Republican, and ex-California governor Ronald Reagan was elected the fortieth president of the United States in a landslide over the incumbent, Jimmy Carter.

Reagan had four children. One, a son named Michael, was adopted while Reagan was married to his first wife, actress Jane Wyman. They also had an older daughter, Maureen. The other two—a son named Ron and a daughter, Patti Davis—were the products of his union with second wife, actress (and former first lady) Nancy Davis.

Soon after his father's election, Michael Reagan found himself in a pickle. Hoping to sell shares in an investment partnership, he invoked his father's name in promotional materials, the language inferring that by participating, investors would have access to the president and his administration. Of course, President Reagan had no knowledge of or connection with the scheme. Caught in a storm of criticism and threatened with censure, if not prosecution, Michael abandoned the effort and looked for a cause that would both raise his profile and his bank account in a more appropriate manner. He found it in powerboat racing, of all things, and before I knew it I found myself in the thick of things with a new best friend, the president's erstwhile son.

Reagan, in cahoots with some professional fund-raisers, approached Anheuser-Busch with a bold if not extraordinarily coherent idea for the company to leverage its involvement with the 1984 Olympics. Reagan and a crew of two others would attempt to break the record for a speedboat traveling up the Mississippi River from New Orleans to Saint Louis, a distance of slightly more than one thousand miles. Their sleek, specially outfitted craft would be adorned with Olympic logos and that of the Bud Light beer brand. At the end of the run, Anheuser-Busch would host a gala $250 per plate benefit dinner at the Marriott Pavilion Hotel, just two blocks from the finish line. The featured speaker would be none other than Michael's father, the Great Communicator.

It fell to me and the agency to organize the PR for the run and to handle the invitations and logistics for the dinner. News conferences were held hours apart in New Orleans and Saint Louis to announce the forthcoming assault on a record that was so obscure almost no one knew it existed.

A couple of weeks later, Regan and his crew set out in their $250,000 twin engine thirty-eight-foot Wellcraft boat. A little less than a day later, they reached Saint Louis, chopping hours off the old record. Their welcoming party included August A. Busch III, hotel baron J. Willard Marriott Jr., and the president of the United States. A couple of hours later at a sold-out dinner, President Reagan bestowed a special Olympic achievement medal on Mr. Busch, after which he held the audience spellbound with tales from his pre-Hollywood days as a young athlete and sportscaster, linking athletics generally and Olympic competition in particular with the essence of America's greatness.

As the dinner wound down, a triumphant Michael Reagan meandered over to me and asked, "Did you have a chance to meet my dad?"

"Not exactly," I replied rather modestly. "He's been pretty busy and so have I."

"Well, come with me," Reagan said, leading me over to where his father was accepting best wishes from some of the VIPs on hand.

"Dad, meet Joe Finnigan. We have him to thank for making this a tremendous success. He's one of us. You should try to get him on your staff."

"Well," he said characteristically, and with that the president of the United States beamed and shook my hand. A couple of weeks later in the mail I received a photo of the handshake. Unbeknownst to me, a White House photographer captured the moment. It was inscribed, "To Joe Finnigan with sincere thanks for all your help.—Ronald Reagan."

The dinner raised nearly $300,000 toward Anheuser-Busch's Olympic commitment. In a post-event briefing session at the brewery, I told a contingent of marketing folks, "Mike Reagan may be a rascal, but he has more energy and creativity than most, and he makes good on his promises. He's a good guy." (Years later, Michael Reagan would find a measure of prominence and relative respectability as an author, Republican strategist, and host of a conservative syndicated radio talk show.)

Forty-Five

Just when I thought I'd been involved with almost everything imaginable in the product marketing and promotional realm, I was summoned to the office of Jack MacDonough, who at the time was the brewery's vice president of brand management. "When's the last time you tried to break the sound barrier?" he asked, tongue-in-cheek. "It's been a while. Why do you ask?" I replied, equally facetiously.

A one-time Cornell University rowing team member and Stanford MBA, MacDonough was a razor-sharp, self-styled wheeler-dealer who liked to rub shoulders with celebrities but preferred to fly under the radar. He was about to sign a deal with movie-stuntman-turned-film-director (the late) Hal Needham to sponsor an attempt to break the sound barrier *on land.* "It's been tried before, several times, but no one's pulled it off. Some science guys don't believe it's possible. The best part is that if Needham's unsuccessful it won't cost us a dime. If they succeed, we owe him a million bucks. What do you think?"

"Er...tell me more."

"Needham's in cahoots with some tech types with credentials up the wazoo. They have a needle-nosed, jet-powered tricycle they want to call the Budweiser Rocket. Needham has a guy who's crazy enough to try to drive the thing—a fellow movie stuntman named Stan Barrett who, by the way, grew up here in Saint Louis, as did Needham. They'll soon be ready to run at the Bonneville Salt Flats. Publicity—lots and lots of media coverage—will be key. That's where you come in."

I'd worked closely with MacDonough in the past and knew I could speak candidly. I also knew Hal Needham—by reputation: his *Smoky and the Bandit* movies starring a younger, dashing Burt Reynolds had been smash box office sensations a few years earlier. Never mind that the critics considered them cinematic travesties.

"Jack, whether you have to pay Needham or not, if this attempt falls short, at the very least it will embarrass the company. If worse comes to worst and this guy Barrett crashes and gets killed, it'll play some real havoc. You want publicity, and we can get it. But I'm not sure you need it, and there won't be any smoke screens or excuses if it blows up in our faces. By the same token I know you well enough that we better get ready to generate the press coverage as well as preparing for other contingencies. So what the hell, huh?"

The mission team set up shop in the Utah desert and began their runs in the bright red torpedo-shaped vehicle. Before long they were achieving speeds in excess of 600 mph. Soon enough, however, they discovered that the topography of the salt flats was too soft and mushy to allow the vehicle to go much faster; it actually got bogged down in the terrain. Undaunted, and having attained a degree of credibility as their speeds increased, they moved to the firmer footing of the dry lake bed at Edwards Air Force Base, California—one of two landing strips for NASA's latter-day space shuttle flights. Ironically, the new site was immediately beneath the wild blue yonder in which Chuck Yeager, the legendary test pilot, first broke the sound barrier in a Bell X-1 aircraft in 1947. In fact, Needham convinced Yeager to join the effort as a technical advisor, adding legitimacy and interest to the caper.

The speed required to break the sound barrier fluctuates with the elevation, or relationship to sea level, as well as atmospheric conditions. At Edwards AFB, the Bud Rocket team ran faster and faster; they estimated they'd need to exceed 725 mph to reach their goal. Finally one fine December morning Stan Barrett fired his rocket and the bright-red missile shot forward, its speed documented by air force radar and telemetry. About midway down the course the vehicle began to shimmy wildly, its rear wheels came off the ground and waves—presumably sound waves—were visible through camera lenses and to the naked eyes of some spectators. But there was no sonic boom. Then in a few seconds with its speed continuing to increase the buffeting stopped. When Barrett finally popped his chute and came to a stop the instruments had him at 739.666 mph. He had set a new land speed record and broken the sound barrier!

It triggered an exposure bonanza for Budweiser—television commercials, a broadcast documentary, tons of press coverage, a nationwide tour for the rocket car and more. Even so, the effort spawned a debate, albeit an obscure one, that probably continues to this day. The achievement was forever marred by curious radar readings, the absence of a sonic boom, and Needham's refusal to adhere to a two-run protocol established for such attempts. Their ace in the hole, for what it was worth: a letter from General Yeager proclaiming that the speed had been reached and the sound barrier broken. The Budweiser Rocket today resides at the Talladega Raceway Museum in Alabama, and an exact replica was donated with considerable fanfare to the Smithsonian Institution.

Hal Needham got his million dollars, and Jack MacDonough his money's worth and then some. Plus he got to rub shoulders with some Hollywood types. But I couldn't help but wonder if it was worth it, given the risk, the ubiquity the Budweiser brand already enjoyed, and an overall lack of athletic or social relevance. That was another matter altogether.

(MacDonough would later leave Anheuser-Busch to join Miller Brewing as president. Ultimately he was elevated to the chairmanship and then pushed out.)

Forty-Six

For many years Coors "Banquet" Beer, "brewed in Golden, Colorado, with Rocky Mountain artesian spring water," had extraordinary cachet, mainly because it was available only in the twelve westernmost states. That began to change, however, as Coors's distribution expanded eastward, and the company elected to lock horns more and more with Anheuser-Busch and other brewers.

When asked in light of that development if he might build breweries elsewhere in the United States given the importance of its legendary Rocky Mountain water source, then Chairman William Coors said publicly there were no such plans, adding however that they could brew their beers almost anywhere. Consumers and industry watchers alike were left scratching their heads on that one.

Then Mr. Coors, who'd always enjoyed a good relationship with August Busch III, ran ads in major newspapers claiming that due to the malt toasting method used in the production of his beers, Coors was the only major American brand free of nitrosamines, which had some dubious cancer-causing connection. Coors disclosed the information in full-page ads in major daily newspapers after telling industry counterparts he would not try to exploit the situation, the value of which was questionable at best in the first place.

Industry watchers thought Coors's behavior was due to mounting pressures—concerns over softening sales and fading image. Coors was no longer the top seller in California, Anheuser-Busch having vaulted into the lead there in the late 1970s. Moreover as the company extended distribution to the rest of the country and as more and more consumers tasted the product, it lost much of its luster. "Colorado Kool-Aid" detractors called the exceptionally light-tasting brew.

Knowing Busch III felt stung by the double cross and hearing scuttlebutt that some of Coors's newer local distributors were disillusioned after investing huge sums in their operations, I conferred with a colleague, David Garino, who'd spent many years with the *Wall Street Journal* and who still had excellent contacts with the influential national business and financial daily. We approached *Journal* bureaus in Dallas and Chicago and found significant interest in a possible story on the disenchanted wholesalers. Thanks to tips from well-connected Anheuser-Busch field sales representatives, we were able to provide the publication with the names and phone numbers of a list of restive Coors distributors. The next step was to sit back and let the reporters do their jobs.

Ultimately the story appeared on the front page of the *Wall Street Journal* on a crisp October day just as an Anheuser-Busch national sales convention was getting underway in Los Angeles. It was a blockbuster, as the disgruntled Coors wholesalers who were spotlighted did not try to sugarcoat their fears and frustrations. As I arrived at the auditorium where the convention sessions were held, there were literally dozens of A-B faithful walking around with copies of the Coors story in hand. Small groups of them were huddled together animatedly pointing at the piece, laughing, and giving one another high fives. The timing, while coincidental, was perfect.

Later that morning during a break in the proceedings, August Busch III spotted me and waved me over. "What do you know about that story in the *Journal* this morning?" he asked.

"I know it's a great piece, one that takes another chunk out of the Coors mystique."

"You know what I mean."

"Why, August, I have no idea what you're talking about," I replied, a twinkle in my eye and a smirk on my face.

"Nice piece of work, whomever it is we have to thank," Busch said.

I had come to love committing gotcha PR.

Forty-Seven

Kathy attended that Los Angeles sales convention with me. It was five days of unadulterated, yet controlled, bacchanalia—lavish cocktail parties and dinners separated by brewery pep rallies—general sessions featuring a galaxy of entertainment and sports luminaries, designed to promote even more fervent worship at the altar of the iconic, majestic A & Eagle. It was some five years after the outbreak of Beer Wars, and Anheuser-Busch had successfully thwarted all pretenders to the throne it had occupied in regal fashion since the early 1950s. So it was time to exhale and celebrate.

As we prepared to head back home, the Saint Louis Cardinals were in the thick of the postseason playoffs. "You know what this means, don't you?" I asked. "More parties—several of them every night. I don't know if my liver can survive."

The Cardinals did survive—the playoffs, that is, and went on to face the Milwaukee Brewers in the World Series, which they won in seven games thanks to the split-fingered relief pitching virtuosity of Bruce Sutter, the heroics of rookie centerfielder Willie McGee, and the canny leadership of manager Whitey Herzog

• • •

The following spring with the World Champion Cardinals in Saint Petersburg, Florida, for spring training, I got a call at home one evening from Judy Carpenter Barada, the administrative assistant to Herzog, who back then was the power behind the ball club's front office throne.

"We need you to call Whitey down in Saint Petersburg and get him to apologize to Jack Herman and his managing editor," she said, obviously agitated. Herzog and Cardinals broadcaster Mike Shannon had been out to dinner, got into their cups a bit, and decided to pull a prank on one of the reporters covering the team. They picked on Herman, the old *Globe-Democrat* beat writer, as he was considered the most gullible of the press corps regulars and they knew where to find him. When they got back to the hotel, there he was holding court as usual in the lobby with some impressionable Cardinals fans from up north.

They got a table in the hotel bar and invited Herman to join them. Flattered by the invitation and with his guard down, Jack was only too happy to oblige. "We've traded Bruce Sutter to the Mets for so-and-so and a player to be named later," Herzog confided, "and we wanted to be sure you weren't blindsided by it."

Herman couldn't leave the room fast enough. His paper was on deadline at the time, and he knew the best he could do was phone in a squib. He'd do a more full-blown story the following day. He returned to the bar. Herzog and Shannon were still there. "Thanks, fellas," Herman said. "I owe you one—I was just barely able to get something in for tomorrow morning's paper."

"You've got to be kidding," Shannon said. "Surely you didn't believe us. We were just having some fun with you. There's no trade."

This time Herman left the room faster than the first. By the time he reached his editor the next day's paper was on the press, which had to be stopped and the front page made over, resulting in a two-hour delay in deliveries. Managing Editor George Killenberg was blind with rage—first with Herman for falling for the hoax, and then with Herzog and Shannon, the perpetrators.

Herzog was anything but repentant when I finally reached him. "If the son of a bitch is that stupid to fall for it, he deserves whatever he gets.

For Christ sake, he didn't even ask one question of us. Some reporter he is..."

"Whitey, we need you to apologize to Herman and his managing editor," I said, gulping big time. Herzog barely knew who I was, much less with whose authority I spoke, if any.

"The *Globe*'s been a great friend and booster to the Cardinals and the brewery," I told Herzog. "We need this to happen." We went round and round, but Herzog wouldn't budge, probably figuring that as one of Gussie Busch's favorites no one could make him—never mind the old man's gin rummy playing relationship with the *Globe*'s publisher, Duncan Bauman, which I did not fail to mention.

I gave up and focused my attention instead on Shannon, who by then was back in his room. "Mike, it's important that either you or Whitey apologize to these people. We don't want Killenberg or Bauman to go to August or Mike Roarty. They don't want or need this. Neither do you." That did the trick. The last thing Shannon wanted was to stir up the powers that be; his job was not that secure as second banana to the great Jack Buck, who in those days was not always Mike's staunchest ally.

Ultimately Shannon saw to the apologies. It was not the same as if it had come from Herzog, but it got the job done, and Shannon was grateful to me, whom he assumed could have had a hand in making his broadcasting career briefer than it should have been.

In 2010, Whitey Herzog was inducted into the Baseball Hall of Fame.

Forty-Eight

April 7, 1933 marked the repeal of Prohibition. It was also the grand debut of the Clydesdales, the majestic draught horses of Scottish descent that over time became a world-famous symbol for Anheuser-Busch and its flagship brand, Budweiser.

The Clydesdales were a surprise present celebrating the enactment of the Twenty-Second Amendment from a thirty-four-year-old Gussie Busch to his father and namesake, August A. Busch Sr., who'd heroically kept the company afloat with other business ventures during the Great Depression and the thirteen-year great social temperance experiment that failed. Scores of other US breweries were not so fortunate.

Fifty years to the day later, octogenarian Gussie Busch stood near the epicenter of the vast brewing empire, his son August III at his side. It was a perfect crisp, clear early spring day. A marching band played the familiar, rousing Clydesdales' theme song. And the eight-horse hitch, resplendent in its black leather and gold tack, its bright-red Studebaker-built beer wagon in tow, began the short trek up Pestalozzi Street to a reviewing stand where both Busches and assorted VIPs waited to wish them well. In one block the strapping geldings went from one national historic landmark, the stables…past another, the Gothic brew house…to a third, the old schoolhouse building that later became the company's headquarters.

Busch III read a congratulatory message from President Ronald Reagan, who called the horses a national historic treasure in their own right, and then gave a brief overview of the hitch, its history, and the company's commitment to their breeding and continuation of the bloodline. A toast and other remarks followed and the VIPs adjourned to lunch in the executive dining room.

In orchestrating the reverie we'd also arranged extensive national media coverage, including a satellite video feed to all Anheuser-Busch installations coast to coast and numerous television news operations. Plus we spearheaded publication of a commemorative coffee table book entitled *Here Comes the King*, which became a best-seller for Viking Press, and thirty years later remained a popular item at brewery and Busch Gardens gift shops and other retail establishments.

• • •

Beginning with the 1982 World Series, the right field wagon gate at Busch Stadium flew open before each postseason game and the Clydesdales came galloping out as "Here Comes the King," their rousing theme song, blared away over the public address system. Invariably the crowd went wild. Old Gussie Busch, clad in a Cardinal red blazer and matching western hat, would ride atop the beer wagon waving to the fans as it made several passes around the field. It was an enormously popular ritual, and superstitious Cardinals fans believed it brought the team good fortune.

That luck, if any, almost ran out during the 1987 World Series when the driver of the hitch lost his bearings. The wagon, with Gussie aboard, got too close to the elevated pitcher's mound and began to tip over. Fortunately forward momentum brought the rig back to all fours, and the frail, eighty-eight-year-old beer baron somehow managed to keep his seat. August Busch III saw the incident from his field box perch, his mouth wide open the entire time. The following evening the hitch had a new driver; the previous one having been exiled to clean the stalls at the Clydesdale stables in New Hampshire, if not a gulag in Siberia.

• • •

That incident and the Cardinals' success in the 1980s notwithstanding, August III never seemed comfortable as a team owner. By 1985 shortstop Ozzie Smith, Garry Templeton's replacement, was making $3 million annually en route to the Baseball Hall of Fame in Cooperstown, New York. The thought of that and some of the other Cardinal salaries drove Busch III to distraction. Never mind that Smith was regarded as the slickest fielding shortstop ever to play the game and, through hard work and dedication, he'd become a fine hitter. The Cardinals made it into the World Series that season. In the playoffs they defeated the Los Angeles Dodgers when Smith, a switch-hitter not known for his power, corked a dramatic walk-off home run, the only one in his career batting left-handed. (The feat was immortalized by Jack Buck's "Go crazy, folks!" call, considered by many to be the signature play-by-play example of the Hall of Fame announcer's storied career.)

A colleague was a fly on the wall the following morning when Mike Roarty asked his boss, "What do you think of your three-million-dollar man now?" "We/pay/the/man/to/hit/the/ball," Busch III reportedly responded with a clipped snarl. End of discussion.

As time passed Busch III also could not abide the ongoing criticism to which he and the company were subjected by the press and rank-and-file Cardinals fans when the team sputtered. "We don't need the aggravation and the lack of appreciation considering everything the company has done for this city," he thought. So in 1996, seven years after the death of his father, Gussie, the Cardinals together with the rest of the Civic Center real estate holdings were sold to an investment partnership headed by William DeWitt Jr. for a reported $150 million—a steal by any definition. (*Forbes* magazine valued just the baseball piece of the deal at $1.6 billion in 2016, seventh best among Major League franchises.) It is worth noting that the present owners have done a wonderful job with the Cardinals. They have been in the 2004, 2006, 2011, and 2013 World Series, winning two of them, and their emphasis on developing young talent has paid off handsomely.

Forty-Nine

Speaking of the Clydesdales, there's an old saying in brewery circles—they look great in a parade, but they're hell to clean up after.

For many years those who were given the job of managing the hitches often found themselves in the crosshairs of senior management, Busch family members, wholesalers, and at times even the organizers of the many local pageants and parades at which they appeared. Sometimes simultaneously. It was a thankless job, and only the most savvy men and women survived the experience; there were only three hitches, and the poor souls who scheduled their appearances frequently found themselves pulled every which way but loose.

One especially prickly situation arose a short time after the company had finished locking horns with the Reverend Jesse Jackson. Busch III's half sister Carlotta, based then in Pasadena, California, had for many years been the driving force behind the so-called City of Saint Louis entry in the venerable Tournament of Roses parade. There was always a theme for the parade, and the float, made entirely of flowers, was always pulled by the Clydesdales. The cost of the entry was paid for by Anheuser-Busch—always with the blessing of August A. Busch Jr.

On this particular occasion Lotsie, as she is known, had submitted an artist's rendering of the proposed entry for the following year's parade. Actually it called for two floats—a big one in front pulled by the Clydesdales and another smaller one behind pulled by a team of all-black miniature ponies. The people riding on the lead float would all be dressed in white from head to toe. Those bringing up the rear would be made up in blackface—a la the Al Jolson movies of the 1920s—and would be in all-black attire. The theme: "Me and My Shadow."

But Busch III was running the show now, not his father, and when he and Denny Long saw the rendering they sensed potential trouble. Then August and Denny flagged me down and asked for my take on the idea. I took one look at the drawing and advised them that there was only a 100 percent probability that it would beget a hailstorm of criticism and grief. "*You* tell Lotsie," they insisted, and within minutes I was speaking with her on the other end of a conference call as Messers. Busch and Long sat silent, probably expecting an explosion. I did not know Lotsie well. But I did know that as one of her daddy's little girls she was not used to being told no, and that she'd been allowed to design the Busch Gardens facilities in Van Nuys and Houston that were commercial flops (unlike those in Virginia and Florida) and which had since been bulldozed to make room for brewery expansions. So I approached the assignment with considerable trepidation. I took a deep breath and tip-toed through the details of brewery's recent set-to with Jackson, which may or may not have been news to Lotsie given the rarified air present in the circles in which she traveled. Thankfully, she got the idea right off and agreed to go back to the drawing board, literally, and come up with something more acceptable. Whew!

While all was well that ended well, the incident underscored something I encountered more than once in dealing with people of privilege: birthright does not necessarily prevent cluelessness.

(Now well into her eighties, Lotsie is today Carlotta Busch Webster. She resides in Palm Beach, Florida.)

Fifty

The end came with astonishing suddenness.

In October 1983, I took a call from a Houston-based *Forbes* magazine reporter who was doing a story on how beer is brewed. He said he planned to key on Coors's brewing process, since the Colorado brewer did not pasteurize its product and, he said, other major domestic competitor's beers were not as naturally brewed, which is not the case. He also planned to contrast certain US brewing practices with those of some prominent European producers. He wanted to speak with someone in brewing at Anheuser-Busch.

Sensing both a possible mine field and an opportunity, I told the journalist, apologetically, that I could not cooperate with him because of the hatchet job his publication had done on old Gussie Busch and the company after the one-hundred-day labor stoppage six or seven years earlier. I added, however, that not only did *Forbes* have it wrong on that previous occasion, they were confused this time around too. So I said I'd mail him some information on Anheuser-Busch products—the ingredients used, the brewing process, and other relevant background. The package contained only existing material approved for public and news media consumption, most of it prepared in the wake of the earlier nasty Beer Wars skirmishes with Schlitz and Miller. The reporter thanked me, and that was that.

However, knowing that brewing and product quality were sacrosanct with Busch III, and since the inquiry was from *Forbes,* I called his office to advise him of the contact and how I'd handled it. Big mistake. He exploded. "Dammit, Joe, I told you never to have anything to do with that magazine. Never." I'd taken a risk and it backfired.

"August, you don't want this reporter going off half-cocked, doing an article on brewing with no input from the industry leader. There's just too much room for inaccuracy and mischief." Busch of course remained unimpressed with my reasoning.

Realizing I was in big trouble, I tracked down John Graham and told him what had transpired. Later that afternoon Graham discussed the matter with Busch and told me that, as feared, after nearly (at that point) ten raucous, rewarding, and result-filled years, my days with Anheuser-Busch were over. Never mind the decade-plus of loyal service or the many, many doubles, triples, and homers I'd had a hand in on the company's behalf. It was over. Just like that. I'd sensed potential trouble coming and thought, given the constraints, that I'd handled it the best way possible. My mistake was telling Busch about it, although that may have only forestalled the inevitable given the aftershocks of the Chelsea debacle.

"This could be the best thing that ever happened to you," Graham said, trying to put a positive spin on it and to show support for a long-time partner. "You can start fresh and concentrate on building new business; you were probably on the A-B account too long for your own good anyway." On the one hand, I was relieved—I was beginning to feel a bit stale and, after all, I was still a senior partner at Fleishman-Hillard. The idea of testing my skills in other areas did have some appeal. At the same time I was devastated—my heart, soul, and ego were completely invested in Anheuser-Busch and, back then at least, if you worked at Fleishman-Hillard and did not work on Anheuser-Busch you were not a first-tier player. I understood that better than anyone; the first tier was my creation.

The following day, Graham met with Busch III and outlined the agency's plans for the future leadership of the account. Two vice presidents—Jim Morice and Paul Siemer—both of whom had cut their teeth in part on my Beer Team, were talented, extremely capable, and had solid experience with the client—they would be elevated to executive vice presidents. Morice would head the corporate, public, and industry affairs of the A-B business, Siemer the brewery and beer marketing piece.

Nevertheless I came a cropper. What was I going to tell my wife? My kids? How would I appear to the people at work, where I'd been such a big shot? For the next six weeks—all the way through the Thanksgiving and Christmas holidays—I was in a tailspin, doing very little work, opting instead to isolate, feel sorry for myself, fret about the future, and drink way too much. I was grateful to Graham and bitter toward Busch III, who I felt may have been looking for an excuse to send me packing ever since the Chelsea kerfuffle. Regardless, it was not fair, not right, and not revocable. I knew the score, but all I could think about was a decade's worth of loyalty, devotion, and the results—success after success, an incredible record of achievement that counted for nothing. That said, I did not see myself a victim, but I sure as hell was glad I never took Denny Long up on his offer to become an Anheuser-Busch employee.

Before the dust had settled I got a call from brewery vice chairman Fred Kuhlmann, with whom I'd been at odds or in hot water on numerous occasions.

"I'm sorry this happened, and just want you to know that I did not have a hand in it," he said rather curiously, referring to my exit from the account. On the other hand, Mike Roarty asked me to his office for a face-to-face expression of appreciation for my work over the years. And surprisingly, I did not hear from Denny Long.

When the *Forbes* article that triggered the incident finally appeared, Busch III reportedly asked all too typically, "What's the big deal?" The materials I sent the *Forbes* reporter apparently helped convince him that there was not much to the story; the result was a watered-down piece, the gist of it being that different brewers went about their craft in different ways.

• • •

When the axe fell, I was neck-deep in Anheuser-Busch's attempt to build a new brewery in Fort Collins, Colorado. Curiously, the proposal met with stout opposition from some locals whose objections may or may not have been fanned by Coors, accustomed as they were to having their home state to themselves. Incredibly, the local opponents maintained a brewery in the area would lead to increased alcoholism in the community and environmental chaos. They claimed too it would play havoc with the hourly wage structure, since brewery jobs paid three or four times the going community average.

A referendum was scheduled to decide the matter. It had to do with the annexation of the proposed plant site into the city limits linked to a tax increment-financing package that would provide critically needed utilities for the project. When the company's vice president for engineering and construction, Barry Beracha, learned I was on the way out, he went to Busch III and said, "If we want this plant built I need Finnigan to continue ram-rodding the project. He's a key player, and we're too far along to risk a change now."

"So use him," Busch replied. Thus provisionally reanointed, I would run the Fort Collins campaign for the better part of two more years. In the end the measure passed, and construction on the Fort Collins brewery was cleared to begin. Afterward, Beracha sent me a letter expressing his thanks and spelling out what he felt I contributed to the effort, specifically citing energy and strategic savvy—with a copy to August A. Busch III, from whom—no surprise—there was no further word.

• • •

I'm asked often nowadays for a perspective on how in 2008 Anheuser-Busch could have fallen prey to a bold, hostile takeover by InBev, an international brewing company with headquarters in Belgium and a senior executive corps comprised mainly of wealthy, extremely savvy Brazilians.

The short answer is that A-B got fat, happy, and was ripe for the plucking. It's my considered belief that the company began to lose its way beginning some two decades earlier, back in 1987, with a slow, almost imperceptible decline that started with the departure of Dennis Long. (Two of Long's key underlings were caught, convicted, and went to prison for taking kickbacks from a vendor—federal offenses. See chapter sixty-two.) Alas, with Long out of the picture there was no one in the senior management ranks to serve as an effective alter ego to the CEO—someone with the courage and credibility to push back, balance out, and fend off the influence (or acquiescence) of a cadre of largely inept sycophants who populated those positions. Theirs was to do the bidding of Busch III, who was imperial, arrogant, and insular with an astonishingly narrow worldview—a gaggle of empty suits that he had made fat, rich, and risk-averse as time marched on.

Ironically, for a time Busch III worried that the Seagram Company would try to make Anheuser-Busch a part of its spirits empire, but that threat, if it ever was one, petered out years earlier when young Sam Bronfman decided he'd rather be an entertainment mogul and moved his company's focus in the direction of Hollywood.

Over time A-B tried its hand and failed at an astonishing number of non-beer ventures—soft drinks, wine, snack foods, cruise ships, restaurants, retail baking, a theme park in Spain, and more—all entrusted to the hands of several key executives who were part of the company's so-called policy committee—to say nothing of its true Achilles heel, the international expansion of its core beer business. (Less than a decade earlier, A-B could rather easily have acquired the international assets of the group that ultimately became InBev but backed off—another blown opportunity and a classic example of the company's institutionalized fear of risk.)

Eventually, as Busch headed toward retirement he installed his son, August IV, to run the company, and things went from middling to worse. The scion's checkered past, playboy reputation, and widely rumored substance abuse battles caused eyebrows to be raised and breaths to be held in the industry, the company, the local community, and on Wall Street, casting doubt on his prospects for success. And at each turn, when he attempted to put his imprint on the organization, he reportedly was thwarted by his father, who remained the dominant A-B board member. (Paranoid as this behavior may have been, a good guess is that Busch III feared his son would do to him what he'd done in the mid-1970s when he ousted his own father as CEO.)

So with its stock wallowing in the forties in the face of a perfect storm of economic and political circumstances, the canny Brazilians of InBev were able to put a financing package together, and Anheuser-Busch was theirs for some $52 billion or $70 a share.

It remains to be seen whether the boys from Brazil have the proper DNA to succeed in the beer business *at this level.* So far, so good, it appears. They have proven to be effective cost cutters plus product innovators and marketers, and they have put a huge dent in the debt they took on to buy A-B; more recently they have moved on to make a $100-plus billion acquisition of SAB/Miller, their nearest competitor. With that deal complete, AB/InBev is by far the largest brewer in the world.

(A definitive, blow-by-blow account of the epic end of an independent Anheuser-Busch may be found in *Dethroning the King: The Hostile Takeover of Anheuser-Busch, An American Icon,* an authoritative 2010 book by former *Financial Times* merger and acquisition beat reporter Julie MacIntosh. Likewise, *Bitter Brew,* a 2012 book by former *Los Angeles Times* reporter William Knoedelseder, provides an insightful and rather juicy look at the Busch dynasty and the family that ruled it for five generations.)

Book Two

Fifty-One

Still reeling after the changing of our agency's Anheuser-Busch guard, my first break and a slim measure of redemption came soon thereafter with an invitation from Ralston Purina to step in and rescue a major pet food promotion.

Bob Hillard had done some work over the years for Ralston at the corporate level, but despite numerous tries, the agency had not penetrated the brand management side of the business—the marketing sector where the real projects and budgets were. The breakthrough came out of the blue with a call from the product manager for Dog Chow, a top-selling flagship brand and category leader. The previous year Dog Chow sponsored a nationwide contest called "Search for the Great American Dog." It made strategic sense, but the results were disappointing based on entries, media coverage, and sales impact," she stated. "We're convinced the program has potential. We've parted ways with the agency that handled it last year. You've done some great work for Anheuser-Busch, and we're hoping for some of that same magic over here," she amplified.

We reviewed the promotion and within a few days returned to Purina's Checkerboard Square headquarters with a plan and a team of people to make it happen. We recommended stretching it to a nine-month promotion. At key intervals, the company would select state then regional champions; each would get strong publicity support. Five regional finalists would be flown to New York, and the winner—the dog receiving the most votes from the pooch-loving public—would be announced. The top dog would be the toast of the town for a day or two. There'd be a news conference, a ride on the Purina Macy's Thanksgiving Day Parade float, appearances on several network talk shows, interviews with the wire services and *People* magazine—the works.

The people's choice was a Springer Spaniel and its owner a cute twelve-year-old girl from the Midwest. They were perfect in every respect—clean-cut, well mannered, photogenic. Their picture would appear on several million bags of Dog Chow, and the little girl's parents planned to use the $25,000 prize money for her college education.

Overall, the Dog Chow people were quite pleased. Entries, media coverage, voting, and sales were way up. However, in classic MBA fashion, they whined that they were growing tired of doing it and complained further that they paid Fleishman-Hillard $600,000, big money in those days for an agency project fee. I countered that the promotion was the talk of their company and the grocery trade and that it had all the ingredients to become a classic annual event. It was pure Americana, and they owned it. They relented, electing to renew with us for at least one more year.

John Graham weighed in: "I told you getting away from the brewery would be good for you," he insisted.

"If you like kissing your sister," I rejoindered, recalling that he could be a wee bit patronizing on those rare, somewhat awkward occasions when he didn't quite know what to say, which didn't make him wrong.

So after years of trying, Fleishman-Hillard had broken through at Ralston Purina. And when we entered the project in the PRSA Silver Anvil competition it won, making it two Silver Anvils for me in three years in the coveted marketing communications category. I was proud of both of my Silver Anvils but, while it may not have seemed so at the time, the second one was especially important because it signified that I may have been down after Anheuser-Busch, but I wasn't out. I still had game.

• • •

I took advantage of every opportunity to acquire stock in F-H, and had almost everything riding on the belief that if we were ever going to become financially independent, this was the ticket. Kathy thought I was crazy, but I thought nothing of borrowing $25,000 or $50,000 at a crack from Boatmen's Bank to buy shares in the firm at the prevailing book value of $2 or $3 each. In time, abetted by a number of stock purchases and splits, I became the firm's number two shareholder, second only to Graham, and in due course those loans were paid off.

Fifty-Two

The three things I liked most about agency life were playing the role of hired gunslinger—the outside expert who comes swooping in to save or make the client's day; the thrill of the new business hunt—from program inception to the final presentation, especially competitive shootouts against other firms; and the idea that you never knew from one moment to the next where or when your next big opportunity might come. But come they certainly would, of that I was confident. Over time I had also grown supremely confident of my ability to sell clients or prospective clients on whatever program we were proposing for them.

Case in point: a visit I got one day from a marketing consultant for Liggett & Myers Tobacco. He'd heard about our work for Anheuser-Busch and Ralston Purina and thought it was just what his client needed.

The Durham, North Carolina-based company—at that point no longer a major player with once-big brands like Chesterfield, L&M, Lark, and others—had found a profitable new niche and a fresh lease on life in the generic cigarette category. They were on the hook to spend a couple of million dollars to sponsor the main entertainment venue, an open air amphitheater on the banks of the Mississippi River, at the New Orleans World's Fair, and they wanted major public relations support for the investment.

When I took a look at Liggett's contract with the exposition, it seemed like a reach strategically. "All they're getting for their money is some signage, an inanimate slab of concrete with a roof over it, and seating for five thousand people. Different entertainers will perform there daily, and we won't be able to call on them for anything, so what do we do?" I asked during an agency brainstorming session.

Then it hit me: "There may be a way to bring the amphitheater to life, figuratively speaking. We need to find someone through whom we can connect Liggett & Myers with the facility and the acts appearing there. We need to find ourselves a host—an official, designated master of ceremonies to represent Liggett—welcoming audiences and performers, and when he's not doing that he'll be making news himself. We'll get him lined up for feature stories and interviews so he can discuss his involvement with this project along with other experiences. I know just the person, a perfect candidate for this role, if we can get him," I said.

"Who, pray tell?" asked a colleague.

"Bert Parks."

Best known as the toothy, longtime host of the Miss America pageant, Parks had been fired unceremoniously from that job several years earlier. He'd worked in broadcasting for decades—first in radio and later in television as the emcee of quiz shows and other programming. In fact, I recalled, one of Parks's yesteryear sponsors was Old Gold cigarettes, so the idea of working for a tobacco product might not be objectionable to him. He'd also become somewhat of a cult figure and an accomplished comic actor in his later years, appearing on television on shows like *Saturday Night Live, Night Court,* and in a classic guest shot on the sitcom *WKRP in Cincinnati* as the erstwhile father of the station's irrepressible sales manager, Herb Tarlek.

We tracked Parks down. He was in his midseventies, living in virtual retirement in Hollywood, Florida, but flattered to be remembered and intrigued with the idea. Just as importantly, he was still keen mentally and seemed, at least in preliminary discussions, to be a genuinely nice guy—someone the agency and the Liggett people would enjoy working with. We fashioned a personal services contract calling for Parks to make twenty appearances during the course of the fair, some on-site as the facility's official host, with other days devoted to visiting major markets for interviews, during which he'd talk up Liggett's amphitheater sponsorship and the fair.

For the day-to-day operation of the program, I recruited Dave Senay, a bright, young account executive who came to F-H from the PR staff of his alma mater, Saint Louis University.

It was no coincidence that the fifth anniversary of Parks's dismissal from the Miss America pageant would occur during his work for Liggett, enhancing his allure as an interview subject. Also, it would mark five years since the Miss America crown had been stripped from Vanessa Williams after nude photos of her were published in *Penthouse* magazine. For sure Parks would have plenty to say about both incidents when the time came.

Parks relished being back in the spotlight. He and Senay clicked, and he enjoyed New Orleans immensely. On several occasions, he and a platoon of agency and Liggett executives dined at one of the town's five-star restaurants, enjoying the Cajun cuisine for which the city was famous, followed by extended "training" expeditions through the French Quarter. Despite his age, Parks could more than hold his own with his youthful entourage, and he thoroughly loved it when other revelers recognized him.

In the end, Liggett & Myers was delighted with Parks and with Fleishman-Hillard for recommending him to solve the somewhat knotty problem their World's Fair sponsorship represented. Unlike so many celebrities I encountered over the years, Parks proved to be a genuine, down-to-earth fellow, a pleasure to work with.

• • •

Later we would work for Louisville-based Brown & Williamson Tobacco, taking on assignments for their Kool cigarette brand and other products. That relationship ended, however, when F-H decided as a policy matter to do no further business with tobacco interests—but not before the top executives of each company in the industry testified under oath at a Congressional hearing that their products were not addictive and that they did not cause cancer and other life-threatening diseases. Jeffrey Wigand, B&W's whistle-blowing head of research and development, would ultimately debunk those claims, a courageous move that played havoc with his personal and professional life.

Fifty-Three

As time passed and the humbling aftereffects of the fall from favor at Anheuser-Busch preyed further on my psyche, I became less and less comfortable in my own skin. Accelerated drinking amplified my occasionally caustic personality, an increasingly erratic work performance, and a somewhat diminished passion for the job, and I knew it. So I decided to do what any good chemical-dependent might try before the jig was up: control my drinking and try to lighten up... become less heavy-handed...be an all-around nicer guy. But under no circumstances was I going to lay off the sauce altogether. I thought of it as "exorcising the asshole factor." Deep down, however, I knew it was merely window dressing, and it wasn't enough—at least not if I was honest with myself about tackling my real issues or ruining my health altogether.

I needed to do that because I wasn't ready to go all the way, even though at some level I understood its inevitability. In the meantime, I rationalized, "I can still hold my own professionally."

• • •

"What's happening at the brewery?" The question was from C. J. McCarthy, my uncle and godfather. "I'm not involved with that company anymore," I replied, sorry I'd responded that way and refusing to go into detail because it was late and C. J. was on his fourth or fifth Jim

Beam on the rocks—nothing new there—and I didn't need the barely coherent, sour, avuncular input it most certainly would have triggered.

The youngest of my mother's four brothers, Cornelius James Giblin McCarthy was perhaps the saddest character I ever knew. After a World War II hitch in the navy that took him all the way to San Diego, he was to have been the next generation doctor in the family, but he flunked out of Providence College's premed program and never looked back. Eventually he enrolled in a junior college and became certified as a medical lab technician.

"What happened; I thought you were in there tight with the brewery?" he slurred. "It's a long story and it'll keep," I assured him. "Don't worry; I'm up to my eyeballs with other work."

C. J. was an embittered loner and a confirmed bachelor until age forty-two when one night in a tavern in Saint Louis he hooked up with Frances Bacon, a twice-divorced fellow lab tech who hailed from Mississippi and who could match him drink for drink. Sixty days later they were married. She was tall, scrawny, and shrill with a complexion like exposed aggregate, poorly disguised with drugstore makeup, but he loved her. She made him happy, and they shared a common obsession—barhopping. Sadly, less than a year into their marriage, she fell ill. The diagnosis was cardiomyopathy, a virus that attacks the heart muscle. Three months later she was dead.

After that, C. J moved back to Springfield, took a job with the Memorial Hospital pathology lab, and went doggedly about the business of feeling sorry for himself, making the rounds of the same seedy joints where for him it all began years earlier—spewing acerbic about everything and everyone to no one in particular. One Saturday night at one of his regular haunts he got so sloppy drunk the bartender sent him home in a taxicab. The cabbie dumped him out at his seventy-five dollars a week residence motel, but instead of turning in for the night to sleep it off he decided to walk back to the tavern to get his car. It was a two-mile trek under a pitch-dark sky on an unlighted stretch of blacktop back road. When he was about halfway to the cocktail lounge a young man doing about 60 mph in a pickup truck came over a rise and didn't see the pedestrian whose stupor had vectored him almost to the middle of the road. He was killed instantly. Besides a twinge of obligatory regret about my uncle's passing, it made me angry. Clearly, both C. J. and I suffered from the family disease. It was the elephant in the living room all over again, reminding me of all my other aunts, uncles, and cousins with the same affliction and the lengths to which they'd go to act as if nothing was wrong. "He *didn't* have a drinking problem and that *wasn't* what killed him," one of the McCarthy aunts said at the funeral home when I mentioned it. "It was that damned twenty-year-old delinquent driving double the speed limit. I hope he rots in jail forever for what he did to our brother," she said. "No self-respecting member of this family would say otherwise." Never mind that there'd been no charges filed as a result of the accident, and never mind that if that incident hadn't killed him it was just a matter of time before the poor, pathetic SOB bit the dust some other way. But at age forty-nine his number was up. I knew I had a number too. We all do.

Fifty-Four

"Roses are dead,
Violets are through,
Season's Greetings
From your favorite Jew."

As his greeting card one holiday season reflected, Wayne Charness's wit was almost as well-honed and widely acclaimed as his rock solid reputation as one of the Big Apple's top publicists. In addition to our professional relationship, my New York protégé and I became fast friends. I stayed at his West Seventy-Second Street apartment on business trips to New York—the apartment from which one October Monday evening out his window he viewed the slain form of John Lennon on the sidewalk outside the ex-Beatle's Dakota condominium. In turn, Charness visited my family at our lake house and became good friends with Kathy and our sons.

But several years with Fleishman-Hillard in New York left Charness with an acute case of professional wanderlust. He eventually moved on, and after a brief stint with two other agencies, moved to the corporate side, making his way to Pawtucket, Rhode Island, and the Hasbro Toy Company where he flourished. Shortly after joining Hasbro, Charness called to say the company was looking for agencies for its various lines of toys, games, and children's accessories. Capabilities presentations would take place in New York City, coordinated by a consultant friend of CEO

Stephen Hassenfeld's. The fellow looked and behaved like a cross between Truman Capote and Rip Taylor, and his qualifications for presiding over the tryouts were never clear. More than thirty agencies were invited to the cattle call, ensuring mass confusion and little else.

Yet we made the cut, and F-H was invited to compete for a specific Hasbro assignment. A team headed by myself and Bob Keating, then general manager of our New York office, arrived early to present their ideas for the program at Hasbro headquarters, a renovated A&P grocery store. We were asked to wait until Hassenfeld finished a prior meeting. It lasted virtually all day. He finally appeared, promptly put his head down on the table, and left it there, making no eye contact with the agency people and remaining silent and almost lifeless for the duration.

We won the business anyway and worked for Hasbro for many years. Steven Hassenfeld died of complications associated with AIDS not long after.

(Wayne Charness retired from Hasbro after twenty-eight epic years on February 28, 2014.)

Fifty-Five

Honda Motors became a Fleishman-Hillard client in 1983. I was not involved with the initial courtship or the early work on the account, much of which centered on establishing a presence in Washington, DC, and capitalizing on the startup of the company's first US assembly plant in Marysville, outside Columbus, Ohio.

Several years later, however, Honda announced plans to introduce a second, more upscale and technologically advanced line of cars in America to be called Acura. When Honda asked F-H to assist with the introduction of its new Acura "channel," as they called it, John Graham asked me to make it happen.

Since most of the company's Japanese higher-ups had difficulty with English and for other related reasons, it was decided an American executive should serve as primary spokesman for the rollout. The choice was Senior Vice President Cliff Schmillen; he'd spent thirty years with Honda, mainly in sales, and was an excellent choice for the role. He was distinguished in appearance, courtly, likeable, quick-witted, and knowledgeable.

Our team met with Schmillen, developed some basic message points, drilled him in the fine art of interviewing, and put together a twenty-eight market whistle-stop media tour coinciding with the introduction of the new car line. The other two leading Japanese auto companies, Toyota and Nissan, were introducing new upscale product lines at almost the same time—Lexus and Infiniti, respectively. But Honda was first to announce and first to have cars available for sale in their new dealerships, and Honda arguably had the upper hand in terms of an existing image as a manufacturer of quality automobiles for the United States and world markets.

Schmillen's platform: Japan, led by Honda with the Acura nameplate, would be going head-to-head with established European luxury carmakers on US soil, the most important and coveted of all markets.

His first stop on tour was an appearance on NBC's *Today* show. As it turned out, he was pitted opposite Bjorn Ahlstrom, president of Volvo/ USA, a smug, contentious Swede with a thick accent and a superior air who insisted Japan's upscale initiative was doomed to fail. Schmillen remained composed as he jousted with the Volvo executive, winning the exchange hands down, citing Acura's positive early road test reviews and advance sales orders while touching lightly on the competitive vulnerabilities of the European makes.

The tour lasted seven grueling weeks, during which Schmillen gave nearly 150 interviews. By the time he finished the early success of the Acura line appeared assured. And Fleishman-Hillard still uses the video of Cliff's *Today* show appearance to demonstrate the dos and don'ts of interviewing in media training sessions for clients and staff.

• • •

NameLab, a consulting firm specializing in developing names for products, services, and companies coined the term "Acura" for Honda Motors. Based in San Francisco, NameLab was established by a former Silicon Valley ad agency head and linguistics aficionado, Ira Bachrach.

Elfin, witty, and urbane, Bachrach and the story of how he came up with the Acura name, I felt, would make for an excellent publicity campaign extension—a sort of second wave in support of the venture and an excellent fit strategically as it would be aimed at consumers who, market research revealed, may have been unsure of the pronunciation and meaning of the term, not to mention that the new Honda line existed.

I sold Honda on the idea, and a fifteen-market tour was scheduled. Delighted to be able to promote his own business and at the same time help a good client, Bachrach openly discussed the process and techniques he used. It involved breaking words down into their basic components or morphemes. (The term "Acura" had to do with design and engineering precision.) Bachrach was a hit on tour, and Honda was once again delighted with the results.

Fifty-Six

When Fleishman-Hillard opened a Washington, DC office in the mid-1980s, one of its charter clients was the Tobacco Institute, the powerful and embattled trade association funded by all but one of the major cigarette companies.

Besieged with health-related concerns, a Tobacco Institute staff member stumbled on a scientist who she thought could help the industry gain some traction in the debate, particularly with a prickly collateral issue—the effects of secondhand smoke.

The scientist was a Scotsman named Gray Robertson whose Northern Virginia-based firm, Clean Buildings, Inc., surveyed the ventilation systems in office buildings for mold, mildew, and other allergy-breeding and respiratory problem-causing factors. His firm was paid to diagnose and cure what he called "sick buildings." Robertson claimed that from his experience there was virtually no evidence that residual smoke caused any workplace health problems. The Tobacco Institute staffer reasoned that if the organization could help Robertson tell his story, activists trying to restrict smoking in the workplace would fail, and industry lobbyists could use the ensuing press coverage to punctuate their arguments with policy and lawmakers. However, she wasn't sure how to proceed, so she turned to F-H.

Aware of our many successes with media tours—most recently on behalf of the Acura automobile rollout—Washington office general manager Rick Sullivan asked me to fly in to discuss a possible similar effort with Robertson for the pro-tobacco interests. After meeting with the glib

Scotsman, the purpose of which was to get a better understanding of him and his story, I told our DC colleagues the idea had real potential. Their concept was to embark on a program with Robertson, centered on an ambitious national media tour schedule, as if he were the client. In other words, his connection with the Tobacco Institute would remain undisclosed even though the Institute would be underwriting the initiative. "You get the program started and teach us how to do it, and we'll take it from there," Sullivan said.

I was happy to oblige, but raised two major caveats. "First, I hope Robertson is the real deal, that his credentials are legitimate in the event some reporter checks him out. He must be able to defend his science," I warned Sullivan and one of his top lieutenants, Paul Johnson. "And perhaps of almost equal importance, I hope you'll be ready if and when someone discovers that the Tobacco Institute's bankrolling this campaign." My colleagues looked at me as if I'd lost my mind. "There's no way that can happen," they tried to assure me. "Look," I said, "this is Washington. This town runs on gossip, leaks, and special interest agendas. I don't even work here and I know that. All it's going to take is one defector or a leak from this agency, from the Tobacco Institute, or from Robertson's own outfit, and whatever progress you make will be nullified; you'll have a real mess on your hands. Sooner or later there's a good chance of that happening, so if you're smart you'll proceed accordingly."

My team got the program up and running and it was proceeding apace. Robertson was a relatively easy sell to news media in the markets initially targeted, and he proved to be a good interview. Eventually it was time for the hand-off to the Washington staffers who kept the campaign moving smoothly for a while. However, as time passed the Tobacco Institute became less guarded about its relationship with Robertson and his firm. He gave TI-sponsored seminars to vested interest groups, wrote op-ed pieces and letters to editors, and even testified in hearings on proposed smoking restriction ordinances. Partially driven by despair, apparently, the Tobacco Institute grew careless, triggering an uprising by antismoking activists that brought the effort to an abrupt halt. With two sets of handlers—the agency and the Institute—F-H lost control, and it came back to haunt both parties in the form of exposure in the news media and legal action by antismoking groups.

The *Washington Post* published an expose; Fleishman-Hillard was implicated and publicly embarrassed. For a time it remained to be seen if the damages would be limited to that. The firm eventually ended its relationship with the Tobacco Institute and decided to engage in no further work in that industry, both because of the Robertson fiasco and to assuage employees who'd grown uncomfortable with our tobacco work.

Fifty-Seven

Washington was the fifth jewel in the Fleishman-Hillard crown, and the world was beginning to pay serious attention to F-H as we opened offices, attracted top talent, and collected clients and awards with impressive regularity. The firm's hardscrabble Midwestern roots and values oftentimes proved a compelling advantage in competition with other agencies. John Graham and the other senior managers—even those in the East and West Coast offices—played that card masterfully, singing the anthem in pitch-perfect harmony: "We're an anomaly. Most of the other major agencies are East Coast-based. They're top-heavy, bureaucratic, and bogged down with internal politics, and the junior people whom they're billing at senior level rates do all the work. With us, what you see is what you get. Our senior people roll up their sleeves and do the heavy lifting, giving you the best strategic thinking, creativity, and overall work product. The proof is in the working with us—and the results," Graham crooned.

He shrewdly modeled the firm's operations after two dissimilar but remarkably successful organizations whose management he admired and had access to—Emerson Electric, a Fortune 500 electronics conglomerate and Wall Street darling, and Bryan Cave, Saint Louis's largest and most influential law firm. Both organizations squarely put extraordinary emphasis on planning, centralized financial controls, operating autonomy for branch offices, and a relentless pursuit of organic growth through new business and, when warranted, new offices.

Financial controls were paramount. The firm had been on shaky ground in the early, go-go 1980s when our focus was on clients' needs and keeping up with our growth. Due to an inept or distracted chief financial officer and blundered external auditing, Graham, Harry Wilson, and I were forced to pledge our homes as collateral to secure a line of bank credit to keep the agency afloat. At one point, symptomatically, an accounting department clerk embezzled $103,000. After that a new CFO, Royce Rollins, was hired, a different auditing firm retained, internal controls established, and thanks largely to Rollins and the improvements he instituted, within a year the firm's fortunes were reversed and the bank debt retired.

At the same time despite a significant string of new business successes, I could not put my Anheuser-Busch experience entirely behind me. I was often testy, despite vowing to lighten up, and my drinking continued to escalate. Nevertheless, I played key roles in opening the firm's New York and Los Angeles offices, and threw my hat in the ring to spearhead recruiting in advance of the opening of an office in Chicago, my old stomping grounds from college and Ogilvie Administration days. That office opened successfully in 1990 when we lured Jack Modzelewski away from Golin Harris, a fine Chicago-based agency.

Fifty-Eight

Our senior managers met each fall to plan for the coming year. Usually we convened in a nice but accessible resort location such as Scottsdale, Tucson, Santa Fe, or the Florida Keys. One year, however, the meeting took place in Cancun, Mexico. Big mistake back then.

Cancun was too distant and its communications substandard in those pre–cell phone days given the needs of the agency's key operatives, all of whom were on hand and had to remain in touch with their offices and major clients during the four or five days they were out of the country. So they were unusually restless.

Entering the Cancun meeting, Bob Keating was on shaky ground as general manager of the firm's New York office. The office remained unprofitable, although only marginally so after the pudgy, red-faced Keating had been in the post for several years; his perennial "we're about to turn the corner" mantra was wearing thin. So his colleagues considered him fair game, and a virtual feeding frenzy ensued.

Keating found Christine's, a disco that did not get going each evening until 11:00 p.m. That's when the beautiful people came out to play. The club's lights went out, the entire place began to quake, smoke engulfed the dance floor from who-knew-where, and the music thundered—threatening the countenance of anyone over the age of thirty-five. There in the midst of it all each evening, glassy-eyed and with a weird grin on his face, was short, squat, well-over-thirty-five Bob Keating, who thought he'd found nirvana.

On our last night in Mexico, the agency contingent went for a dinner cruise on Cancun Bay onboard a motorized replica of a Spanish galleon. Sensing Keating's vulnerability, I told him as we stood on the deck of the vessel that several people were out to get him. Fearing he would be thrown overboard, Keating spent virtually the entire evening with his arm wrapped firmly around one of the stout guy lines suspended from the boat's mast.

Earlier that evening I'd just left my room and was walking up the hallway toward the hotel lobby when I overheard a couple arguing in their room. The man was clearly enraged at his wife's behavior. He accused her of making time with another fellow. "Marcia, I've had it," he said. "You've been coming on to that son of a bitch all week. As soon as we get home I'm filing for divorce." I could not hear the woman's response, if one was offered. Later that night, after the dinner cruise, it was all quiet in the hallway as I returned to my room. In the spirit of "Get Bob Keating" I returned to my room, took a piece of hotel stationery, and wrote: "Marcia, same time tomorrow by the ruins. Can't wait." I signed it "Bob," gave Keating's room number, and slipped it under the embattled couples' door. (There was a Mayan burial mound on the hotel grounds.)

I heard nothing further of the winsome Marcia and her troubles, but I did see Bob Keating the following morning. It was getaway day, and he was pacing back and forth across the hotel lobby in his stocking feet. Seems he'd lost his shoes and had no idea where he'd left them.

Less than a month later Bob Keating and Fleishman-Hillard parted company.

Fifty-Nine

Michael Shanahan, a businessman determined to join the ranks of Saint Louis's civic and corporate aristocracy, was the chief honcho of Engineered Support Systems, a company that produced a range of essential equipment for the modern military—items like air-conditioned portable buildings for officers, movable mess halls, water purification systems, and the like—almost everything today's fighting forces need but for the weaponry. He took his company public, retaining F-H to generate positive buzz prior to the initial public offering. The agency placed several excellent stories in some national business publications, including an especially strong piece in *Forbes.*

At the same time Shanahan also chaired a partnership formed by local companies to acquire and operate the Saint Louis Blues of the National Hockey League, thus assuring that the franchise would remain in the city. And the Blues needed a promotions campaign.

Impressed with the work Fleishman-Hillard did on behalf of his company, Shanahan wanted the agency included among those being considered for the Blues' marketing account. However, the team's chief operating officer in those days, a blithering Irishman named Jack Quinn, wanted no part of F-H for some reason. When Shanahan discovered that the COO had ignored his request, he put the agency search on hold. At that point, we were invited into the competition. Our presentation was so strong Shanahan hired us on the spot, unilaterally, as Quinn looked on speechless. When my F-H team and I met with Quinn a few days later to discuss startup details, he reached in his desk drawer and produced a four-page letter from the head of another agency in town, complaining vociferously that Quinn had hired his outfit and then reneged.

"What am I supposed to tell these people?" Quinn asked.

"Jack, tell them you screwed up the search process by ignoring the instructions of your boss and now you're stuck," I said. (I had no use for double-talkers and considered him *summa cum laude* in that department.)

We nevertheless went to work on the account and were about to unveil the new promotion campaign for the coming Blues season when I got a call from Quinn inviting the entire account team to his office. When we arrived, the duplicitous Irishman made a big production of presenting me with a check for the first month's work. "This is the start of what promises to be a long, wonderful relationship," Quinn gushed as a photographer snapped a picture of the presentation. I felt more than awkward about the situation but thanked him. Then I told John Graham about the incident, queer as it was.

A week or so later, Graham was attending a Cardinals game in the Fleishman-Hillard skybox at Busch Stadium. Jack Quinn was a guest in the box next door. Seeing Graham, Quinn began ragging him over the railing that separated the luxury boxes, regurgitating the saga all over again, punctuating his remarks with complaints that the agency was charging the hockey team too much—more than the firm he wanted to hire originally.

Graham, who'd heard enough, said, "Well, Jack, you're going to get your wish. We quit. Good luck telling Mike Shanahan about this."

• • •

As it turned out, Quinn must not have had much trouble explaining things to Shanahan. Not long thereafter, Mike's company got some bad press in a couple of major financial publications. Choosing to ignore the fact that now-public Engineered Support's financial performance had incurred a reversal and failed to meet Wall Street expectations, he blamed the agency for the coverage and that ended the relationship.

(In time, Shanahan was run off as Blues chairman by the corporate interests that controlled the hockey team and replaced by one of their own executives. However, with the capable and charismatic but previously distracted Shanahan focused fully on his business interests, and after several canny acquisitions, Engineered Support recovered and became one of the most successful NASDAQ-listed companies, with annual sales of more than $1 billion. The company was then acquired in a $2 billion transaction by a New Jersey-based outfit, but some of its executives, including Shanahan, were indicted for unrelated, alleged stock option backdating violations predating the takeover. Some of them ended up pleading out and going to prison; Shanahan pleaded guilty, received probation, and had to repay $7 million to the new parent company.)

Sixty

Seeking to become much better known, a relatively obscure Saint Louis-based national investment management outfit turned to F-H for help. The firm, Edward Jones, had a unique market niche. Unlike Merrill Lynch, Morgan Stanley, and so many of the other silk stocking firms with their huge overhead offices in big cities and high net worth clientele, Jones's stock-in-trade was single-person offices in smaller, underserved communities or neighborhoods with a mom and pop clientele to match. They were also the fastest growing brokerage organization by far and highly profitable.

I assumed responsibility for the Jones account when the F-H account person who had landed the business left to himself join another investment firm, a Jones competitor.

Our day-to-day contact at Jones was a human resources person who'd had responsibility for PR coordination thrust upon her. As such, she was relatively clueless about the function. After a couple of get-acquainted meetings, I typed her boss, the firm's managing general partner, as a disarmingly smug, officious fellow whose real agenda in hiring an agency was only partially clear. The passage of time ultimately confirmed those impressions, I believed.

Nevertheless, we were delighted with the opportunity and set out to get the Jones story told, targeting the *Wall Street Journal* and *Time* magazine, among other key media. The hook: Jones's extraordinarily successful Wall Street to Main Street orientation exemplified by its literally thousands of storefront offices in smaller communities coast to coast.

Thanks once again to my colleague Dave Garino, the agency first succeeded in pitching a feature story to the *Wall Street Journal*. The *Journal* liked the idea of focusing on one typical Jones broker in a small Midwestern town. We suggested several prospective brokers, and the newspaper's Chicago bureau selected a Jones representative in Paris, Illinois, a small rural town near the Indiana state line. The reporter assigned to write the story spent several days there shadowing and interviewing him.

A few weeks later the story appeared. On a scale of one to ten it was at least a nine by any objective standard. It appeared in the coveted right-hand column of the front page of the paper and was continued on an inside page, running some fifty or sixty column inches in all. The featured Jones rep was a big, heavy-set, hail-fellow-well-met who wore a Stetson hat, chain-smoked, knew everyone in town, and drove a big blue Cadillac. The story made note of those traits. He also boasted in the piece that the previous year he earned more than $200,000-an impressive income for someone in rural Edgar County, Illinois. Upon reading the story, the Jones CEO asked why it described the Paris broker in that fashion. I explained there were two reasons: first, it added color, authenticity, and completeness to the article, and second because it was true—Jones's man in Paris was a big, ostentatious, burly, chain-smoking, Cadillac-driving fellow who liked to brag about his prosperity, wisely or otherwise. Although the article was positive in substance and contained every message point that the agency and client had agreed in advance were important, the CEO had nothing further to say about the story.

Soon the agency arranged for the managing partner to travel to New York for a series of interviews with some other national publications and news services. One of the results was a *Time* magazine article that while not as lengthy was every bit as good as the *Wall Street Journal* piece. The CEO expressed no reaction to it either, at least not to the agency. I couldn't help but suspect his seeming indifference to the coverage, outstanding as it was, was due to the fact that the stories dealt far more with the company and its operating approach than the fellow in charge. "I'm leery of this guy," I told the others on the account.

Then storm clouds began to form. *Forbes* magazine learned of a series of lawsuits filed on behalf of some elderly Jones clients claiming they'd suffered significant financial losses by investing in certain mining and other highly speculative issues the brokerage firm was touting. The reporter requested an interview with the CEO, who insisted the investments were sound. He asked the agency for its recommendation on the matter and was advised to grant the interview, the litigation notwithstanding, because the story would appear with or without his cooperation; it would be his only opportunity to try to provide Jones's side of the story. At the same time we cautioned him that *Forbes* might include very little of his comments, as the publication had a reputation for deciding on the direction and content of articles beforehand, and that this would be a tough piece, unavoidably.

Remarkably, we were able to obtain, sub-rosa, an advance copy of the article four days before it hit the streets, providing an invaluable leg up in formulating a strategy for dealing with the fallout. Entitled "Jonestown," it characterized Jones as a less-than-reputable outfit with brokers of questionable qualifications who preyed on the elderly with shaky investments. We worked virtually nonstop for several days and had Jones well prepared to respond when *Forbes* hit the street the following week.

When the dust settled, in private discussions with the agency, the CEO claimed he'd been assured the story would turn out well if he spoke to the reporter. I maintained, to the contrary, that the agency provided adequate, realistic, and clear caveats and went to extraordinary lengths to get a smuggled advance copy of the story in order to prepare the company to deal with the situation—a feat that by itself was worth every penny Jones paid us.

For its trouble the CEO fired F-H. "He had to have someone to blame it on and to deflect possible criticism from himself and the company," I told the account team. "He's still going to have to face the legal fallout and possibly some tarnish to Jones's image," I noted with no small measure of perverse satisfaction.

Sixty-One

One day a year or so after F-H parted company with Engineered Support Systems and the Saint Louis Blues, I got a call out of the blue from my old pal, team president Jack Quinn. There was real urgency in his voice.

"We need your help," he said. "I tried to reach John Graham and he's not available. About a month ago we met with him and briefed him on a very sensitive problem we were facing and it's surfacing literally as we speak."

Quinn explained that an underage girl babysitter alleged that a star Blues player, Doug Gilmour, and his wife enticed the juvenile to engage in sex acts with them. The girl's parents hired an attorney, and he was about to hold a press conference at almost that exact moment.

"It's a little late to ask for assistance, isn't it, Jack?" I asked.

"Well, several weeks ago we had lunch with your boss and gave him the background. Now we need your help." (F-H presumably was pulled into the matter thusly because the partnership that owned the hockey team at that point was composed of a number of Saint Louis's leading corporations, many of which were agency clients.)

"Graham's in Europe and can't be reached. He didn't brief anyone here about the situation, or if he did I certainly don't know about it. If it was so critical we should have been working on a response strategy long before now," I said, thinking all the while that it was a classic Quinn maneuver to try to cover his fanny, fearing he could be held accountable for bad PR by his bosses—Michael Shanahan and the directors of the franchise-owning partnership.

Quinn added: "There's more to it. The girl's attorney approached us and Gilmour several weeks ago and said he could make the whole thing go away if we'd pay his client a substantial sum of money. We have him on tape. We've turned it over to the Saint Louis County prosecuting attorney, and it looks like his office will be taking action."

"Good. That's exactly where it belongs," I said. "Look, that's attempted extortion, a crime, and regardless this is a law enforcement matter. At most the hockey club should put out a brief statement saying the matter is in the hands of the proper authorities, the team will not be a party to extortion, and there will be no further comment until it's settled."

"Mike Shanahan won't be happy that you're not out here helping us," Quinn interjected, obviously in a state of high dudgeon. "He'll be back in town this afternoon, and no doubt you'll be hearing from him."

"Fine with me. Look, Jack, I just told you exactly what to do. That's all you can and should do. Have your in-house PR person issue a one-paragraph statement and then shut the hell up—and tell everyone else connected with management to do likewise. Of course, you can't control what Gilmour's teammates say, but the smart ones will avoid comment."

Later that afternoon Shanahan called. "You wouldn't refuse August Busch or (Emerson Electric CEO) Chuck Knight if they called with a problem like this," he said.

"Mike," I countered, "First, Quinn called here for help literally as the little girl's attorney was holding a news conference. He knew better—it was a CYA call if ever there was one and a classic Quinn stunt. Remember how he tried to handle the agency selection situation? He can't be trusted. Regardless, I told him exactly what the hockey club should do. Anything else would be inappropriate given the circumstances. Besides, neither Mr. Busch nor Mr. Knight has fired us lately, and you've done that *twice*!"

Doug Gilmour was traded to Calgary a short time later and the case was disposed of. Mike Shanahan ultimately was replaced as chairman of the Blues by the partnership that owned the club. Jack Quinn retired and quietly left town. (Finally, after his hockey career ended, Gilmour was inducted into the NHL Hall of Fame.) No telling if the little girl's attorney was able to keep his law license.

Sixty-Two

I opened the *Post-Dispatch* one Sunday morning to learn that an accountant for the Hanley Partnership, a recently defunct local sales promotion agency, had testified in bankruptcy court that a couple of Anheuser-Busch executives received financial kickbacks and other enticements to channel business to his old firm. While I had no prior inkling of the situation, I was not completely surprised at the allegations—the fellow who headed that agency already had served one prison sentence for taking kickbacks and was widely regarded as a sleazeball. Moreover, even though I'd had no involvement with the brewery for several years, I knew both of the Anheuser-Busch executives rather well—one of whom, Michael Orloff, lived three doors away from me; the allegations seemingly explained some things I'd noticed about his lavish lifestyle. The involvement of the other fellow, Joe Martino, was a total shock.

The brewery announced it was conducting an internal investigation of the charges and that it would cooperate fully with the authorities. August Busch III was livid according to the grapevine, understandably. And of course the executives in question were fired.

Before long a federal grand jury indicted the A-B pair on nearly two dozen counts each that stemmed from accepting gifts of cash, automobiles, home furnishings, providing a nonexistent job for one of their wives, an apartment for a girl friend and, of course, tax and wire fraud connected with the receipt of the various items that were not reported as income.

As a stunning upshot of the scandal, Dennis Long offered to resign as president of the brewery, and his offer ultimately was accepted. While he was not implicated in anything illegal and had played a crucial role in the company's success, the alleged offenses happened on his watch—which spoke volumes about the value Busch III placed on others' contributions, as well as their lives. Although I was no longer associated with the company when Long stepped down, I felt as if a Clydesdale had kicked me in the chest.

The accused executives pleaded not guilty. At their trials they attempted to implicate F-H and other agencies in the mess, claiming they/we had also used elaborate gifts to influence brewery executives. There was a major problem with that tactic, however: The Fleishman-Hillard gifts came "one to a customer" and only at Christmas time with the identity of the sender clearly evident. Nothing was under the table. The gifts certainly were not illegal nor did they violate what was then company policy. Besides, the defendants had no direct involvement with the company's public relations function, to say nothing of the selection or retention of such agencies.

(There was a related, touchy issue: many key A-B executives expected to get increasingly more elaborate, expensive, and novel Christmas gifts from F-H and other agencies, and they made no bones about it. For example, one time just before Christmas an in-house attorney who later became the company's chief legal counsel approached me and said, "Such and such agency sent me this and that for Christmas. Let's see you guys top that!" In short, it had turned into a competition and was completely out of control, extending even to the people responsible for the company's ethics policies and compliance.)

When the trial ended, the former A-B executives were found guilty on three counts each—those related to tax, wire, and mail fraud. Both were sentenced to prison, as were two of their agency coconspirators; they did brief stints in federal minimum-security impoundments and were faced with the prospect of rebuilding their lives upon parole.

For its part, Anheuser-Busch adopted a new, much more restrictive and comprehensive policy dealing with the acceptance of gifts and related favors from vendors.

Sixty-Three

When industry observers and our competitors considered John Graham's abundant talents and strengths, they cited his vision, his intellect, his burning ambition, and his brilliant leadership of a firm that was fast becoming a juggernaut in the public relations business, a key component of which was his ability to surround himself with remarkably talented yet dissimilar managers and to keep them all moving in the same direction despite their well-developed egos, idiosyncrasies, fiefdoms, and in some cases enmity toward one another.

Supremely gifted as he was as a manager, at the same time Graham would take behind-the-back potshots at those in or near the inner circle to one another. "The business has passed her by," he would say about one of the partners. "Too bad he's lost that fire in his belly," he would complain about another. Or, "Look how slowly that guy moves, he's a bum." As the firm's next most tenured partner, I often heard such comments about coworkers. Whether I agreed with the assessments or not, and it was generally hard to disagree, I couldn't help but wonder how serious Graham was, what he may have been saying, if anything, to others about me, or if he rightly was sharing a private viewpoint because he trusted me to keep the information to myself. Then again there was always the possibility that canny boss that he was, Graham was inferring that if those within earshot of such remarks wanted to avoid being criticized they would somehow up their games.

Against this backdrop, Graham came to me one day with a surprise proposition. "I want you to assume overall management of the Honda business and grow it into the seven-figure account it should be," he declared. Responsibility for the Honda business had been in the hands of another F-H partner for several years, and Graham apparently felt that fellow had more or less stagnated in the assignment.

"We need to put some fresh blood and stronger leadership into the mix if we're going to have any future with Honda, and I'm betting you can do it," he said.

I was pleased to get the apparent vote of confidence and the challenge. Yet at the same time I was more than a wee bit on guard. If I'm going to take on Honda I need to make some significant lifestyle changes, otherwise it will be my undoing, I thought, which was where my suspicion (or paranoia) came into play. Alcohol was taking an ever-increasing toll on my effectiveness and my health, and I knew it. I didn't drink in the morning or at lunch, but five o'clock was rolling around earlier and earlier and so were the blackouts—occasional alcohol-induced losses of memory of my actions. For example, my middle son, Brendan, was an all-star offensive guard and captain of his high school football team. I often attended his games so hootched up I was unable to fully appreciate what was happening on the field until the second half, when the effects of the booze began to wane.

I went to Graham: "I need help—gotta get this damn monkey off my back," I confessed. He understood and was most supportive. "I was hoping this day would come. Whatever you need..." he said. A few days later I entered a treatment center and then as an outpatient underwent counseling and started attending Alcoholics Anonymous meetings. I got a sponsor, a savvy veteran who was fifteen years sober at the time and who would call me on my bullshit and who had some simple rules—don't drink, go to meetings, and talk to God. One of his favorite pearls of sponsorial wisdom: "For an alcoholic, drinking is like having sex with a gorilla—you're not finished until she says so." Another of his popular caveats: "We all pick our parents the same way, so don't blame your family for your addiction; you're an alcoholic, pure and simple; that's why you drink too much and can't drink ever again." His advice on how to respond if someone insisted I have a drink with them: "Simple—just tell 'em alcohol aggravates your syphilis."

The speaker at one of my first AA meetings was a former pro athlete who memorably said he was so decimated by his alcoholism that he left town for Kentucky to enter the livestock insurance business in a $30,000 Cadillac and, having lost everything, returned to Saint Louis in a $250,000 Greyhound bus! I counted my blessings and knew I was in the right place. As the old bromide goes, I was sick and tired of being sick and tired. My dry date: September 10.

Fresh out of rehab, I had another reservation about taking on Honda. Andy Woods was the key day-to-day player on the business. He was a talented young account executive, well accepted by the client, whose mother had been a high level statewide elected office holder and a force to reckon with in Missouri's liberal political circles; his father a respected editor on the staff of the *Post-Dispatch.* Graham made a big fuss about Woods when he joined the firm, tacitly signaling to him in effect that it was acceptable to go over his then-managing partner's head directly to the big boss whenever he had a complaint or wanted something. More often than not, Graham indulged him, much to the chagrin of his immediate then supervising partner. Aware of the dilemma, I gulped and insisted that I would agree to take on Honda provided Woods answered only to me, and that any attempt to subvert the chain of command would be met with appropriate response. Graham readily agreed; in fact, he seemed relieved.

Then I squared off with Woods. "You're a genuine talent and a good guy," I told him, "but this fair-haired boy crap—going over your boss's head—won't fly with me. You might have been able to do that with the other guy, but try it with me I'll cut your balls off. Understand?"

"Perfectly," Woods said, squirming slightly.

"Good, then we won't have any problems. Now we've got a lot of work to do. The goal is to triple the size of the Honda account. The way I see it, we'll need to get a lot more aggressive. If we can hit the target we're both going to be stars, and for you that will mean a lot of good things. You with me?

"All the way," Woods pledged, "so let's saddle up."

By the end of the following year—some fifteen or sixteen months later—we'd tripled the size of the Honda account; it passed the million dollar mark in total billings, and I nominated Andy Woods for promotion to partner. My faith in him was well placed. He did not disappoint.

Sixty-Four

I was in my office catching up on paperwork one day in 1988 when the phone rang. The ensuing conversation and its aftershocks would end up rocking me to the very core of my psychic underpinnings. On the line was Randall Foskey, an old Georgia-born friend who worked in PR and advertising for Colonial Williamsburg in Virginia. We hadn't spoken in quite a while. (I'd had a hand in hiring him as the first in-house PR manager for Busch Gardens prior to his going over to C. W., as the restored colonial shrine is known locally.)

"Mind if I ask you a personal question?" asked Foskey, consummate Southern gentleman that he was.

"Shoot."

"Wasn't your daddy killed in World War II?" his terminology again betraying his Southern origins.

"That's right, in Normandy, about a month after D-Day."

"And he's buried over there?

"Yes again. Why do you ask?"

"My wife, Debbie, and I just returned from Europe. As you know I'm a history buff, and while we were in France we visited Normandy; I'd always wanted to visit the invasion landmarks. We stopped at the American Cemetery at Omaha Beach, which, by the way, is an awesome experience. We were walking through the cemetery, looking at the various grave markers when we happened on one that said 'First Lieutenant Joseph T. Finnigan, Missouri, 330th Regiment, 83rd Infantry, July 8, 1944.' That has to be your father, right?"

"It sure is," I said, barely able to disguise the expanding lump in my throat.

"Have you ever been over there?"

"No, I haven't."

"Have you ever seen a picture of his grave?"

"No, I haven't."

"We took some photos, including some just of where your dad is. Would you mind if I sent you a couple of the shots?"

"Not at all. I'd appreciate that very much."

He went on to say he'd send some photos and strongly urged me to visit the cemetery, and I promised him I would try.

Soon an envelope arrived from Williamsburg. I opened it to see a tight close-up of a stately pure-white marble cross headstone, engraved horizontally with the inscription Foskey mentioned in his phone call. I couldn't take my eyes off it.

I was certain my father's sisters had never visited the grave nor had they seen a photo of it. All three were still alive. Likewise, my mother's brothers and sisters, six of whom were living and knew my father, would not have seen it. I had large color prints made and sent one to each, along with a letter explaining how I got them. Two of the Finnigan sisters appreciated the gesture. The sole exception asked why after forty-five years I elected to "reopen those old wounds." Not surprised to get the call, I replied, "Because he's my father, and I had to," certain she would not, could not, comprehend.

I was overcome with emotion and curiosity. Just like that, I went from benign indifference to an all-out obsession with the notion of learning all I could about the man, his life, and the conflict in which he and his family made the supreme sacrifice. After decades of hidebound denial I would never experience a force more compelling and came to realize after all that time that a visit to Normandy was the only way I could ever hope to achieve true closure and acceptance and make amends for decades of feigned indifference.

I spent much of the following winter researching the Eighty-Third Infantry and the Battle of Normandy that followed the D-Day invasion in preparation and hope for an eventual pilgrimage to Omaha Beach and a meeting with the father whose very existence I'd tried for so long to ignore.

That phone call from Randall Foskey would set the stage for my life's greatest journey, not to mention a measure of redemption, and I doubt that I've ever adequately expressed my deep appreciation for it.

Sixty-Five

It was easier to do good work for some clients than others. Take Valvoline, for example. It was another in a string of my significant post-Anheuser-Busch client wins. A unit of Ashland Oil, at the time Valvoline was the third best-selling brand of motor oil behind Pennzoil and Quaker State.

Before developing a communications plan for the Lexington, Kentucky-based outfit, we reviewed its relevant strengths and weaknesses. Its public relations function had been in the hands of its advertising agency before we were invited to pitch the account. Strike one. In a well-intentioned move to break with its refining-linked, commodities-based culture and establish a consumer products division of sorts, the parent company moved Valvoline one hundred miles west from Ashland, Kentucky, to Lexington. However, they stocked the pond with old-timers, all white, all male inbreds who'd come up through the organization, rather than introducing some fresh blood—sophisticated new thinkers with authentic brand management savvy. So not surprisingly, what we found was a hidebound organization with marginal, unsophisticated leadership that was too internally focused for its own good.

The good news was that Valvoline needed and claimed it wanted help, and a next generation of top management was waiting in the wings. So from our point of view, F-H was staring at some possible low-hanging fruit. We devised a comprehensive program for Valvoline and went to work.

Before long, the company's aging, longtime president retired. His successor, John Barr, was a dynamic, tough-minded Canadian who'd had a cup of coffee with the Philadelphia Flyers of the National Hockey League before becoming a top sales executive; he had big ideas for the brand.

We handled publicity for Valvoline's Indy Car program and also created a variety of proprietary and image-enhancing programs, including a widely syndicated automotive advice column under the byline of the company's director of technical services. Also we launched an annual "Poll of the American Motorist," which took the pulse of licensed drivers coast to coast on a variety of topical issues. The survey results without fail were gobbled up by the national news media.

Not long after the agency began working for Valvoline, a race car it sponsored, driven by Al Unser Jr., won the 1992 Indianapolis 500. The agency secured guest appearances for "Little Al" on a number of the TV network morning and late night shows, as well as an in-depth *Sports Illustrated* profile of the driver, whose father, Al Senior, and Uncle Bobby Unser both were multiple Indy winners.

Another major undertaking involved providing publicity support for a Valvoline-sponsored *National Driving Test*, which aired annually for several years in primetime on CBS. We subcontracted a portion of the job to a Hollywood-based entertainment publicity specialist, Jeff Mackler, who came highly recommended by the program's first-year host, actress Lindsay Wagner. Jeff got the program reviewed by critics and included in local programming guides from coast to coast, besides obtaining coverage in *People* and *US* magazines and *TV Guide.*

When Valvoline entered the fast-growing quick lube business, F-H got the added responsibility of providing corporate image and publicity support for the venture—indicative at the time of the company's confidence in the agency.

The main challenge with Valvoline was trying to motivate my people to work on the business, a reflection of the lack of substance and institutional treachery associated with the client and the people with whom we had regular contact. Managers up and down the line were imbued with little more than the superficial thoughts and concepts and catch phrases avowed by such pop pap as *The One-Minute Manager*. For a while the company decided it wanted its advertising and PR agencies to be partners rather than just agencies. When I asked the senior vice president in charge of sales for a definition of partnership, he hemmed and hawed and finally said, "You know—a relationship not just based on the fees we pay you guys."

My reaction: "In other words you want us to comp more of our services to you and introduce you to other clients who may be to your benefit?"

"Well, not exactly, but yeah—something like that," was the best answer he could supply.

"We call that something for nothing," I interpreted privately to the account team. "Hell, we're already writing off a quarter of the time we spend on their behalf now, and very few, if any, of our other clients would have anything to gain from an introduction to these people. Bottom line, when they mention this partnership bullshit we politely smile and nod our heads in assent and go about our business as usual."

Our contact person on the client side was an Ashland/Valvoline lifer who was promoted to vice president during the height of the relationship with Fleishman-Hillard. Elated, he said he owed his advancement to my mentoring and the agency's fine work. Beyond that, however, he was a timid sort with marginal talent and limited credibility within his own ranks, which hindered our effectiveness. At the same time his penchant for internal politics was exceptional, causing me to question his trustworthiness.

I lamented the situation to John Graham. "They challenge us to come up with breakthrough ideas, but it's lip service. We bring them exciting concepts, but they don't act—either because they don't understand them, or they're too timid to pull the trigger." The response was classic Graham: "Then let's get another motor oil, one that pays us more, challenges us more, and appreciates our work."

"What's with those people? We have to laugh at their corny jokes and they don't get ours," observed one of my colleagues.

"You've just put your finger on a much deeper issue, but we have to tread very carefully lest they get the impression we're patronizing them and putting on airs," I cautioned. (Meantime, they were paying us as much as $40,000 a month; the bird-in-the-hand rule most certainly applied.)

My frustration was particularly evident in the wake of a concept the agency developed for them to promote careers in the field of automobile mechanics. Born strategically of a growing manpower shortage in the field and an advertising campaign claiming Valvoline was the number-one choice of certified professional auto mechanics, the concept was dubbed "TOP," short for "Technical Opportunities Program." It called for establishing a fund to award Valvoline special-purpose grants to junior colleges and vocational-tech schools offering courses in auto mechanics, plus scholarships for qualified individuals, especially minorities. It had all the makings of a breakthrough, long-term proprietary initiative for the client.

Asked how much it would cost to implement, we recommended a first year operating commitment of at least $1 million in order to assure credibility and legitimacy, exclusive of PR support, with more to be invested in future years if the program caught on. We suggested that perhaps some or all of the funding might be obtained from Ashland corporate or the Ashland Foundation. The program had that kind of potential, and Valvoline's initial reaction was equally enthusiastic. But then: "There's no question it's a dramatic concept, but we need some time to think about it," we were told, only to have it end up, like so many others, in the graveyard of good ideas. I was forced to conclude with regret that the program was too ambitious for Valvoline. I also wondered if it died because the company had misgivings about being too closely associated with minorities.

Then, after thirteen years, Valvoline put the account up for review. The agency's jaundiced attitude had begun to bubble up in its day-to-day dealings with the client, affecting our ability to do good work and virtually guaranteeing our replacement. The increasingly strained nature of the relationship took its toll on the client as well. To no one's surprise, Valvoline elected to go with a different agency at that point.

Sixty-Six

On the brink of becoming the world's largest retailer, Wal-Mart turned to Fleishman-Hillard for communications and public affairs assistance. Wal-Mart had no prior relationship with a public relations agency, and its in-house people were not up to the growing challenges of the times, much less what lay ahead for the company. So in addition to day-to-day support, we were asked to help find a new, more qualified PR chieftain for the Arkansas-based retailing goliath.

Back in Saint Louis, Graham asked if I had any recommendations for the position. "As a matter of fact, I do: Jay Allen would be perfect for the job. He's a Texan, so he's from that general region of the country, he's smart, low-key, and tough-minded when necessary; he'd be an all-around great hire for them." Allen was a former Southwestern Bell (now AT&T) staffer who'd joined F-H and worked for me for nearly a decade before moving to Nashville to head a trial PR joint venture with a local advertising agency. That experiment wasn't working, no surprise, and Allen wanted out.

Graham balked at the suggestion. "I'm not so sure he'd be a good one for us to recommend. He's independent, outspoken, and can be a bit cantankerous," he said. I was certain Graham could not have gained such an impression of Allen without the input of another partner with whom Graham was close and who'd tried using Allen on another account without complete satisfaction. "Jay would be a great fit in Bentonville. He's down-to-earth, a solid pro, and he's looking for his next challenge," I countered, resisting the temptation to ask him how he came by his jaundiced impression of Allen.

Before long, however, I got a call from Allen who, glory be, said he was interviewing for the Wal-Mart job. He knew I'd recommended him for the post. He seemed appreciative and more than a little interested in the opportunity; ultimately the job was his.

• • •

Later there was another, somewhat similar incident. Mike Shanahan was ousted, and the corporate partnership that controlled the Saint Louis Blues of the National Hockey League and the arena in which they played their home games was looking for a new chief operating officer to succeed Jack Quinn.

Again Graham asked if I knew of anyone who might be qualified.

"Mark Sauer would be a great fit," I said. Sauer worked in Saint Louis as a top front office executive with the Cardinals when August Busch III decided to move him back to the company's theme park group, where his career began. His reaction was unthinkable; he refused to leave the ball club, and that seemingly ended any further chance of his working anywhere in the Anheuser-Busch empire. Then he was hired to run another baseball team, the Pittsburgh Pirates. He was doing well in Pittsburgh when the club was sold to new owners who reportedly had different ideas about how to operate the franchise and had set out to gut the team of its highest priced talent. Word on the street was that Sauer, seen as a member of the Pirates' old guard, was back in the job market when I mentioned him to Graham for the Blues arena position.

"I wouldn't dare recommend Sauer," Graham said. "He left Saint Louis in August's doghouse, and since Anheuser-Busch is a major member of the partnership that owns the hockey club, it's doubtful that idea will fly."

A few weeks later, I was in the men's room down the hall from my office, and who should be in there washing his hands?

"Mark Sauer, what in the world are you doing here?" I asked, almost certain of the answer.

"It's very much on the QT, but I'm interviewing for the Blues job," he said. "The meetings are taking place in one of your conference rooms."

"Good to see you, Mark, I hope it all works out," I replied. A few days later, Sauer was named to be the COO of the Blues and the arena, which today is known as the Scottrade Center.

• • •

The Allen and Sauer incidents were a bit curious and, truth be told, worrisome. Was the boss simply exercising an entitlement of his position, without prejudice, claiming ownership of a positive turn of events? Or could it have been connected with my battle with alcohol, my oftentimes prickly disposition, or chronic irreverence? Regardless of Graham's earlier encouragement and support, I wondered if I was damaged goods in the eyes of my old friend and ally, the agency chairman, to whom I owed a huge debt of gratitude on several levels. Was he exhibiting similar behavior toward other members of the firm's old guard? Whatever it was, I decided to practice the golden rule—namely he who has the gold rules—and to keep my mouth shut about both incidents.

Sixty-Seven

Owing to its position in the community, Fleishman-Hillard frequently is volunteered to provide pro bono support for its clients' pet causes. Perhaps ever the cynic, I insisted that *pro bono* was the Latin term for *bend over.* Nevertheless, from the agency's viewpoint, comp work came with the territory. It was expected. It was a responsibility. And it kept competitors away from many of the agency's prize clients. The firm undertook such free work with the same level of commitment its paying clients received. Generally speaking, the agency did what was expected of it, the project ended, the client was pleased, grateful, and usually able to bask in an intended halo of civic admiration. Yet from time to time unusual and potentially explosive situations arose—situations that carried with them more jeopardy than the client or the agency bargained for.

The 1994 US Olympic Festival was a classic case in point. Sanctioned and staged by the US Olympic Committee, the festivals were held in the United States in years when there were no Olympics. They took place mainly in sports-minded cities and served as a showcase for the nation's athletic prowess while sustaining interest in Olympic sports during those three-year spans between the quadrennial international competitions.

Saint Louis was selected to host the 1994 festival after a spirited bid to secure the event. Working with a group of second-tier civic leaders together with the Saint Louis Sports Commission, Andy Woods produced an impressive bid package designed to win the hearts, minds, and approval of the USOC decision makers. It included pledges from many of Saint Louis's top corporate citizens promising all-important financial and in-kind support for the ten-day festival should the city be selected. Part of the rationale for the bid was based on 1994 being the ninetieth anniversary of Saint Louis's hosting the 1904 Olympic Games, concurrent with a World's Fair, which were centered around magnificent Forest Park and Francis Field on the nearby campus of Washington University. Both were still in existence and available for use as festival event venues.

With Saint Louis's selection in hand, those behind the effort set out to establish an organization to stage the games and handle all of the associated requirements—venue selection, marketing, logistics, housing, transportation, and the like. The steering committee chose as chairman a local real estate developer who was rumored to view the appointment as a springboard to statewide politics. A member of a socially prominent family, he was a marginal intellect with little personal magnetism, judgment, or managerial skill. His first official act was to appoint a president—a full-time, paid chief operating officer on whose shoulders the festival would rise or fall. He selected an out-of-work hotel manager with dubious qualifications and a reputation to match. Little did anyone realize at the time how nearly disastrous that combo would be.

The festival's paid staff was a ragtag group who individually and collectively comprised a calamity spoiling to happen. They approached hiring decisions as if they were doling out government patronage positions rather than selecting qualified people who could do their jobs in the relatively small window of time available. The choice for marketing vice president was a retired IBM sales rep with connections to the city's most powerful black political family and who got by largely on his ability to leverage that relationship. His job was to call on Saint Louis's top corporate interests and reel in their sponsorship pledges—commitments they'd already made in most instances. Truth be told, he did not know where to begin, and it fell to the festival chairman to try to clean up his messes, which was well beyond his skills. The first on-staff public relations director was the wife of the mayor; she was equally inept.

The so-called leadership duo began to feel the mounting pressures of time and their own ineptitude. F-H was seen by guarantors as a safety net that would step in and help the festival weather one crisis after another—resulting chiefly from the selection of unqualified personnel, racial tension, and leadership that did not know which way to turn while at the same time resisting outside assistance.

The situation boiled over when a staff accountant posted one too many racially offensive cartoons on an office bulletin board. The marketing guy, who had arrived at the festival with a hair-trigger psyche anyway, exploded. He went to the CEO and demanded the termination of the accountant, who should have been fired after his first transgression. When that didn't happen, he resigned, went public with his complaints, and demanded the CEO's ouster. Then one of his cousins, a prominent member of the festival's board, resigned, and several other African-American directors followed suit.

I was vacationing at Bald Head Island, North Carolina, when I got a call from a board member—a prominent community affairs executive with one of the festival's leading corporate supporters and an old friend and ally. "What in the world is happening over there?" she asked, referring to the festival.

"Nothing more than a full-scale mutiny with serious racial overtones that's put the entire festival in jeopardy while dividing the community even more than usual," I said.

"That's what we were afraid of," she said. "We need to get it under control, and fast. The USOC folks in Colorado are nervous as hell about this, by the way."

"I'll be home tomorrow. I guess we'll have to start knocking some heads together," I said, knowing it was on our shoulders to get the mess cleaned up as swiftly and quietly as possible. "I need you to get the word out to your boss, to the other corporate supporters, and to the rest of the board that most likely heads will fly and broad axes will bear blood. We can't have anyone—*anyone*—second-guessing us."

"You got it," she pledged.

Back in Saint Louis, it took a couple of days to make sure the stars were aligned correctly for a series of moves that, if they did not succeed, would spell disaster for the Olympic Festival as well as a possible setback for black-white relations in a city already noted for its lack of progressiveness, not to mention my agency's reputation as a skilled troubleshooter.

For openers Andy Woods and I met with the chairman and showed him a draft of a news release announcing the CEO's departure and replacement by Mike Dwyer, president of the local sports commission. Dwyer had a proven talent for details and logistics and, more importantly, he would not tolerate the destructive behavior prevalent among the festival's staff. The chairman was informed that Dwyer would be adding his own hand-selected personnel to key staff positions. "We're issuing this at a news conference later today, and you'll need to be there to introduce Dwyer and field media questions," I told him, and he reluctantly acquiesced.

"If this doesn't calm things down sufficiently you'll need to consider tendering your own resignation," I added.

"There's no way in hell I'm stepping down," he spat. "I'm not a racist, and I don't condone what's happened."

"That's irrelevant," I countered. "Perception and reality are identical in this case, and if the CEO's leaving doesn't settle things down you'll be the one with the bull's-eye on your head. This is about saving the Olympic Festival, not to mention civic face."

Clearly, the chairman would not go quietly. He was still smarting and embarrassed by his inability to raise funds for the event; F-H had to step in and close many of those deals because he had so little credibility with the A-list of the corporate community. He saw his festival chairmanship as a way to gain redemption, if not to set the stage for his real objective—a run for Missouri's governorship.

Dwyer's appointment was as well received as his predecessor's exit, but it did not silence critics in the black community. They continued to allege mistreatment, insensitivity, a lack of minority employees on the festival staff, and a similar shortage of vendors and contractors in the overall composition of the event. The complaints and associated media coverage continued unabated. So we called on Wayman Smith, our old

Anheuser-Busch canny cohort from the Jesse Jackson days. "What do we need to do here, Wayman?" I asked.

"Get rid of your clueless chairman," he replied.

"You know, this problem began when no one from the corporate community cared enough to volunteer someone qualified to run this thing," I offered. "So the movers and shakers at the sports commission were stuck, and since they're not insiders they opted for the guy who took the job because he at least is well-known, and he has a social register ID number tattooed on his wrist."

"Yeah, and he's a laughingstock," Smith said.

With just 120 days remaining before the festival opened, we hatched a plan to name cochairs for the festival—one black and one white; the incumbent chairman would have to step down. Ten days after the ouster of the CEO, Andy Woods and I went to see the chairman and urged him to step aside gracefully.

His reaction: "You can't do this to me. I'm not a racist. I put a promising young African-American kid through Country Day, my alma mater, and he has dinner at my house on a regular basis." (Readers should ignore the non sequitur or that the kid was a star running back on the school's highly ranked football team.)

"Those are generous gestures on your part, and I know this is a tough situation for you and a lot of other people who're involved with this mission, but if you truly care about the festival and its success, not to mention your own standing in this community, you'll stand aside," I said. "If this thing fails, think how it's going to look, not only here but nationally. You owe it to yourself and to Saint Louis to step down."

"I need some time to think this over," he said.

"You have until five o'clock tomorrow," I proffered. "If you can't see your way clear to resign so we can announce it together with our other plans moving forward, we'll have no choice but to position it differently, and that will be seen as a forced exit."

Ultimately he relented, but insisted he'd be calling his own press conference after the festival's announcement at a separate location—to be handled by his own PR people. That way, he insisted, he could tell his side of the story and clear his name. The problem, of course, was that there was no legitimate, defensible side to his story, and we made sure certain reporters covering his news conference knew that and formed their questions and conclusions accordingly.

In the end, the outgoing chairman got very little news coverage. The new cochairmen took office. Mike Dwyer did a masterful job pulling everything together. The festival went off splendidly, virtually without a hitch.

When we met for a post mortem, I couldn't help but note that pro bono work can be riskier and more time-consuming than some paying assignments. "We really earned our keep on this one, boys and girls; the irony is that very few people will ever know it."

A short time later the USOC decided Olympic Festivals weren't worth the trouble and abandoned the practice altogether.

• • •

We nearly failed to make it home alive from Bald Head Island. On our last night there we'd been to dinner with another couple, the Johnsons, who were vacationing and sharing a condo with us. It was the last day of September. The weather that evening was brutal—cold, raw, and the sustained wind off the Atlantic was gusting to more than forty knots. We returned by golf cart to our third floor unit and decided to pack, since we were leaving the following morning. I turned the heat on for a few minutes to take the chill off and then we were to meet the other pair to play cards before retiring for the night. As we gathered in the living area, my friend's wife glanced up at a kitchen skylight and saw something odd and alarming—the sky above appeared pink rather than pitch black. I went to the front door to see what was happening, and the knob was too hot to touch. A full-blown fire was raging just outside. "We've got to get out of here now!" I said, terrified. Our only escape was via the bedroom balcony. If we could access that and then make our way down to the ground there was a chance we could escape. I tried to open the sliding glass door to the balcony, but it wouldn't budge. By then fire was beginning to engulf our unit. With one last desperate heave, the door flew open. But that caused a wave of fresh oxygen to rush through the condo, causing the flames to speed toward us. Our luggage, laid out on the bed, literally began to melt. We had just seconds to get out of there. I crawled over the banister and, thanks to some latticework, was able to climb down to the second level, and then dropped to the ground some ten to twelve feet below. Kathy, on the other hand, at first was afraid to follow. I begged and begged and finally she crawled down to the next level and then fell the rest of the way. At that point we were clear of the building but weren't sure what happened to the Johnsons. They appeared moments later from the other side of the building, having escaped from their bedroom balcony the same way we did ours.

As it turned out the island had only a volunteer fire department in those days, but even a fully equipped department would not have made a difference given the conditions.

We found a safe place several hundred yards from the conflagration when it dawned on us that all our possessions were lost in the fire—no money, no jewelry, no credit cards, no plane tickets, no car keys, no nothing. We had only the clothes on our backs, and two of the four of us had no shoes. We watched the windswept fire grow; ultimately all ten buildings (forty condo units) of the Swans Quarters condo complex burned to the ground, a total loss. Fortunately no one was even injured. It was determined later that the fire started with the in-wall heating unit I'd turned on upon our return from dinner—faulty wiring.

Thankfully the Howells, some caring folks from Charlotte, North Carolina, were watching the mayhem and sensed our predicament. They invited us to spend the night at a house they were renting up the beach, a place owned by *Today* show personality Willard Scott. They gave us shoes, spotted me fifty dollars, and even arranged for our traveling companion, a diabetic, to have insulin delivered from the mainland in the middle of the night. The next morning, back in Southport on the mainland, a locksmith got us in our rental car, and we headed toward the Raleigh-Durham airport. When we told the airline folks what happened they were understanding, and we were able to make our scheduled flight home—suffering from the adrenaline rush and terror of the night before, but ever so relieved to be alive.

Sixty-Eight

Andy Woods stood breathless in my office doorway.

"Code blue! Honda's sitting on a time bomb, and they want us in Torrance, stat," he said.

"What are you talking about?"

As it turned out, a dealer in New Hampshire was having trouble selling the generally popular and successful Acura products, so he decided to combine his Acura operation with that of his domestic Mercury line, offering both from the same showroom. However, that was in violation of his franchise agreement, which called for the Acura brand to be sold from separate, freestanding outlets, so Honda said the Acura franchise would be taken away from him. The dealer filed suit to block the move and in the process testified he'd been forced to pay kickbacks to Honda employees in order to secure needed inventories—preferred models or colors. That triggered an investigation by federal authorities, and no less a media powerhouse than the *New York Times* was onto the story. The allegations, for example, included under-the-table payment of college tuition for one Honda sales representative's daughter and house payments for another. The accusations concluded on an even more alarming note: "If you think this is bad, I can think of a dozen other dealers who'll surface with their own horror stories once this goes public," the aggrieved car dealer swore.

"Wait, there's more," Woods said, somewhat fatalistically. "Several of the company's ranking Japanese executives were scurried abruptly out of the country, and apparently some of the senior American managers will be implicated. In other words, this may not be confined to a couple of rogue sales reps out in the hinterlands trying to pad their personal fortunes."

Woods and I arrived the next morning at American Honda's California headquarters. We were ushered into a conference room and met by the company's chief legal counsel, its human resources director, the in-house public relations manager—all Americans—and Mr. O. Iida, a senior Japanese public affairs executive who'd been posted in Europe and South America before assuming his duties in the United States. It was unclear at that juncture whether the absence of any senior sales officials was significant, but it was conspicuous, we noted privately.

"We have a very serious problem, and we need Fleishman-Hillard to use all of its resources and influence to help us get through it," said Mr. Iida, clearly concerned.

"It would be helpful if we could get briefed on the situation before considering whatever actions may be advisable," I said. Over the next forty-five minutes we received background information and were able to fill in some of the blanks. Among other things we learned the *New York Times* expose was scheduled for publication the following Sunday; we had four days in which to devise a strategy and mount a defense.

As the session wound down, I had one final question: "Are the accused Honda people—those in the field and those who work here at headquarters—guilty of these charges?" With that Mr. Iida announced it was time for a break.

In a hallway during the recess, Iida cornered me. "Joe-san," he said slowly and in a muted voice, "we need your help. This is a very bad situation."

"I understand that, Mr. Iida, but time is short, and if we are going to help we need answers to basic questions. You and Honda should know after ten years and the other sensitive situations that we've been through together that we seek this information only to help the company. The more we know, the better prepared we are to provide the assistance and advice that you need." Iida needed more convincing; to his traditional

Japanese way of thinking, apparently it was a matter of honor maintained or lost, and that trumped everything.

When the meeting resumed, I tried another approach. "I've asked the man who manages our Los Angeles office to join us. He'll be here within the hour. If the *Times* story is running in Sunday's edition, the article likely will be distributed in advance to syndicate-member newspapers. However, those papers won't be able to use it until *their* Sunday editions. (Oftentimes, major stories like this are in the hands of syndicate members several days early so that certain sections of the Sunday editions can be made up and printed in advance. Our man was an ex-editor of a daily LA-area paper who still had excellent contacts there.) He may be able to obtain a copy of the story well before it's published. If so, we'll know exactly what the *Times* story says, and we'll be able to develop our responses accordingly."

After another recess, this time for lunch, our colleague arrived. He had with him an advance copy of the story. It was devastating.

"How'd you get that?" a Honda lawyer asked.

"I can't say. The person I got it from swore me to secrecy."

Everyone in the room seemed impressed and appreciative except for Mr. Iida, who again asked me to join him for a private conversation in the hallway. "I thought when we retained your firm we were engaging a firm with great influence, Mr. Finnigan. Now is the time to use that influence."

"I don't understand," I feigned.

"We cannot have this story appear."

"Mr. Iida, you're asking me to get this story killed. That's impossible. We don't have that kind of influence. No one does. And if we were to try, it would make matters worse, much worse. This is the *New York Times*, arguably the most influential newspaper in the world, the so-called newspaper of record, and the people who run it and work there view their freedom to publish as a sacred right. We would not dare try to subvert that in any way."

"This is not good for our relationship," Mr. Iida said.

With my never-completely-dormant Irish rising, I let rip: "Look, this isn't Japan. Corporate interests in this country do not control the news media. Whenever we begin to ask the tough questions you call a recess. Clearly you cannot or will not tell us what we need to know if we're to help you. Now, we have used our contacts to obtain an advance copy of the story, at considerable risk. If the *New York Times* knew that, there would be even more trouble to deal with. As it is we have a three-day head start to develop our response strategy. I suggest we use this to our advantage and get to work right away. And if that jeopardizes our relationship with the company, I'm sorry—it can't be helped."

We went to work, in close contact with the American Honda in-house public relations manager, who mostly and characteristically remained mired in a fog of indignant denial. "Those dickheads. Who do they think they are?" he said repeatedly while we tried to remain focused on the task at hand. Within twenty-four hours we had developed a crisis plan and comprehensive response materials with scant input from our in-house counterparts. However, they seemed comfortable with the materials, some of which may have needed to be deployed as soon as Saturday evening as the first edition of the Sunday *Times* and other papers came off the presses. That depended in part on how other news media picked up on the *Times* story.

We set up a crisis hotline and were ready for the phones to start ringing. The story was a blockbuster. "Honda's Ugly Little Secret," the headline read; Dorin Levin was the reporter. It was so long and involved, however, it defied easy condensation by other news organizations, including those subscribing to the *Times* News Service—those with a leg up on the others. In a postmortem session to assess the damage on Monday, I noted with relief that we were fortunate the story did not receive wider play nationally. "Certain news organizations either have part-time people working weekends, or they're just plain lazy. This may have helped our cause," I observed.

Nevertheless, before long a handful of Honda sales personnel were indicted, including the company's top American sales executive. During legal discovery, it was learned that the perpetrators' code phrase for their illegal behavior was "passing the football." Ultimately they were tried in federal district court, pleaded out or were convicted of multiple counts of various kinds of fraud, and sentenced to prison. The Japanese senior executives who mysteriously departed for their homeland at the first hint of trouble never were charged.

Woods and I recommended that Honda go on the offensive internally in the wake of the scandal, adopting a progressive new corporate ethics program designed to help guard against a reoccurrence of the problem, to deal swiftly and decisively with violators, and win back any public confidence that may have been lost when the trouble surfaced. That suggestion was ignored.

The bumpy experience with the kickback crisis did not spell the end of Honda's relationship with Fleishman-Hillard, which is not to say it wasn't on life-support. The end came a year or so later when our Washington office made a unilateral pitch for the business of the Motor Vehicle Manufacturers Association (MVMA), a trade group representing the Big Three domestic automakers—General Motors, Ford, and Chrysler. Washington general manager Rick Sullivan did not give me a heads-up on the pitch. But Honda got wind of it, advised the agency it was a conflict of interest, and severed ties with us.

As it turned out the MVMA pitch was successful. Fleishman-Hillard was awarded the business and in the Washington office much celebrating ensued. However, within weeks Chrysler was acquired by Daimler-Benz of Germany and the MVMA imploded. It was a pyrrhic victory to be sure, not to mention that it triggered the loss of a valued long-term client, Honda, wholly avoidable tension between our Washington and Saint Louis offices, agency embarrassment, and blemish on the vaunted F-H reputation.

"See what happens when you mess with us," I whispered tongue-in-cheek to a colleague who'd also had trust issues with F-H Washington. "By the way, remember when I warned them the Tobacco Institute/Healthy Buildings caper could blow up in their faces? Just saying."

Sixty-Nine

For many years, if not now, the true buckaroos of corporate communications were the men and women of the airlines. Actually, there were almost no women in that field even though they rather easily outnumbered men in most other sectors of the PR profession. I figured it was due partly to the swashbuckling nature of the airline industry. Everyone from the CEOs on down seemed to be hypermacho types who never knew from one moment to the next when they were going to suffer a crash and the loss of hundreds of lives, have a plane hijacked, or go tens of millions of dollars into the red due to too few passengers or spikes in jet fuel costs. An entire airline could be wiped out with the events of a single day. It was hard to imagine a more adventuresome, crazy business.

It seemed to me that airline executives were great risk-takers because so many came from the pilot ranks. Many were trained to do what they did in the military—flying fighter jets, helicopter gunships, medivac, and bombers against daunting odds. Frequently this testosterone-rich mixture spilled over to fuel the behavior of many in the PR ranks and other areas of airline operations as well.

Our only previous airline experience had been with a small outfit that flew commuters in and out of Chicago from other parts of Illinois. In 1971, the company lost a plane in bad weather near Peoria. Its CEO was at the controls, and he and half a dozen young State of Illinois attorneys with whom I worked perished in the crash. Twenty years later the same thing happened to a reincarnation of the same airline, only this time the carnage happened near Carbondale, downstate. The pilot was a horny hotshot who'd ignored weather warnings and onboard instrument problems because a young lady awaited him at the end of the line. That time, Fleishman-Hillard was retained to help what was left of Air Illinois through the NTSB hearing process. However, when they worked off an upfront retainer in less than thirty days and did not pay subsequent invoices, we suspended activity. Fortunately, from my point of view, we were out just a few thousand dollars. Nevertheless, I was loath to take on another airline.

But business is business, and years later when Bruce Hicks, PR manager for Continental Airlines, called and wanted to get together, I jumped at the chance. Sort of. Houston-based Continental was one of two carriers operating under the corporate umbrella of Texas Air, a holding company controlled by the notorious Frank Lorenzo. The other was Eastern Airlines, an even more venerable carrier based in Miami, founded by World War I flying ace Eddie Rickenbacker and later headed by former astronaut Frank Borman. Eastern was wrangling with the machinists union that represented a large portion of its employees.

Hicks, the Continental PR manager, had heard of our work during the Beer Wars era—the battle for supremacy in the brewing industry between Anheuser-Busch and Miller. "We need some traditional PR counsel and help with special events," he said, "but our brothers at Eastern need some good old-fashioned hardball and dirty tricks. We expect to be billed for every hour you spend on our behalf." I liked that, but I was uneasy with the preoccupation with mischief that Hicks and others seemed stuck on in early meetings. Besides, Texas Air had a reputation for stiffing agencies. At that point my instincts told me to bail, but John Graham said let's proceed; his reasoning was valid as F-H did not have an airline client, so proceed we did.

Our work for Continental was straightforward enough. The airline emerged union-free from bankruptcy, and F-H helped trumpet new routes and service while preparing a plan to christen the new Continental terminal at the Newark, New Jersey, airport.

Eastern was another story, however. Lorenzo had bumped Borman from the helm of the carrier and was about to file for Chapter 11 protection so as to rejigger its union contracts when the machinists struck. Citing service and safety failures by the cash-strapped airline, the union got the FAA to ground the entire Eastern fleet pending a review of maintenance and safety practices. In a meeting at our New York office attended by a dozen or more airline and agency PR people, Lorenzo's trusted advisor and former FAA general counsel Clark Onstad laughably said, "Boys, let's not shoot ourselves in the foot." Then he proceeded to spend three hours with us captives discussing ways to sabotage the union and its leaders. Scary stuff. Later he unilaterally encouraged his normally reclusive boss to accept an invitation to be interviewed by correspondent Tom Jarrell for ABC's *20/20* program, during which Lorenzo appeared to live up to his reputation as the sinister so-called Darth Vader of air transportation. To put a cherry on the sundae, host Barbara Walters characterized Lorenzo during the broadcast as "the most hated man in America."

In the face of the grounding, we recommended that Lorenzo, flanked by his board of directors and the presidents of Eastern and Continental, hold a tightly scripted, well-rehearsed media briefing to tell his side of the story. Prior to the event, plain-spoken Frank Borman, still an Eastern director with a commanding presence, walked into a conference room where preparations were underway and asked, "Who was the stupid cocksucker who got Lorenzo to do that ABC interview? It was a disaster." For his part, Onstad cleared his throat repeatedly while a half dozen PR people sat mum and squirmy. All I could do was look at Borman and roll my eyes.

The briefing took place in the ballroom of Washington's J. W. Marriott Hotel. It was standing room only with sixty or seventy television crews and more than two hundred reporters on hand. For a day or two, Eastern regained its share of voice in the debate, but before long the machinists galvanized an alliance with the pilots and flight attendants, and Eastern's fate was sealed. The airline was out of business.

By then, Eastern and Continental owed Fleishman-Hillard a combined hefty $1.4 million in back fees and expenses. Bruce Hicks had bailed out at Continental, after which a secretary found a pile of unprocessed agency invoices stashed away in his desk drawer. After several meetings with Onstad, more than one sleepless night, and threats to file a high-profile lawsuit against Texas Air and the still-operating Continental, our CFO Royce Rollins and I agreed to write off $400,000 of the pending balance.

Two years after the collapse of Eastern, Lorenzo tried to form another airline. Ironically he wanted to call it Friendship Air. However, the federal government denied his application, and Lorenzo went home to Houston having ruined several airlines while amassing considerable personal wealth.

Seventy

Following decades of feigned hidebound indifference, I'd become obsessed with the father I never knew and the circumstances surrounding his death in combat. It was triggered by the photos of my father's grave I'd received from Randall Foskey, my friend from Virginia (chapter sixty-four). In the intervening months, I'd spent countless hours in the library and on the Internet researching the Eighty-Third Infantry, obtaining the unit's after-action and morning reports from the National Archives, and reviewing documents and correspondence my mother saved for me.

Finally, Kathy and I flew to London, spent a few days there, and then took an all-night ferry across the English Channel, departing Southampton and landing on the Normandy coast at dawn—just as the Allied Forces had in early June nearly fifty years before. We arrived in Cherbourg, went by rail to Bayeux in the heart of the province, and from there rented a car to visit the American Military Cemetery at Colleville sur la Mer and other World War II landmarks.

I couldn't sleep as we trudged across the English Channel in the cramped, humid quarters of the ferryboat. The excitement and anticipation were excruciating—as if I expected my long-lost father to be there in person to greet us. We stayed at a charming hotel in Port en Bessin, a quaint fishing village between Omaha and Gold, two of the five D-Day invasion beaches. From there the American Cemetery is just six miles west.

As we entered the cemetery by pure chance we encountered the superintendent, a career civil servant, American Philip Rivers. Upon learning that I was both the only son of one of the soldiers buried there and a first-time visitor, Rivers couldn't do enough for us.

The cemetery sits breathtakingly on a steep cliff overlooking Omaha Beach and the channel, its beauty and solemnity befitting one of the most hallowed places on earth. More than 9,300 Battle of Normandy casualties are buried there amid immaculate grounds, the marble crosses and Stars of David marking their final resting places—all facing west, toward home, in perfectly symmetrical rows.

Rivers ushered us to Plot E, Row 26 almost at the midpoint of the 170-acre site. As we turned up the row toward grave twenty-three, I noticed a floral arrangement at the foot of one of the markers seventy-five or one hundred yards distant; somehow I knew it was my father's. "1 LT 330 INF 83 DIV Missouri July 8 1944," the engraving on his cross read. Arriving at the spot, I fell to my knees, embraced the three-foot-tall marble cross and, out loud, announced myself and Kathy. For the next two hours tears flowed as I variously stood, sat, and knelt there, speaking intermittently. I realized this was physically as close to my father as I would ever be, and that I was the only member of the immediate family to visit the grave. Finally, I wrote a note and stuck it in the sod next to the marker. It read: "For Mom and the others, we came to honor, respect, and love you. I beg your forgiveness after all these years."

Eventually, we returned to Rivers's office. He gave us a map charting the day-to-day movements of the Eighty-Third Infantry in early July 1944 and urged us to visit the area where my father was killed. I asked where the flowers at the grave came from. Rivers checked his records. "They were from a Mr. and Mrs. Randall Foskey of Virginia," he said. Once again, I was overwhelmed emotionally.

From the cemetery, we drove west and south into the bocage—the Normandy hedgerow country. We found it unimaginable that so many American and German soldiers had been slaughtered in the pastoral surroundings. More than one thousand years old, the hedgerows are impenetrable stands of vines and brambles from four to ten feet high and four to six feet thick, dividing fields and providing relief from the relentless English Channel winds. In the summer of 1944, heavy rains and intentional German flooding created a sodden marsh that made the going almost impossible for the US soldiers—deadly conditions the Allied military planners failed to anticipate fully.

Armed with Rivers's map and a forty-five-year-old letter from my father's chaplain, I guided our small Renault through the lush, serene countryside dotted with picturesque villages and names like Sainteny, Saint Andre de Bohon, Tribehou, Saint Georges, and Hottot. As we reached the intersection of two rural routes—D97 and D29—I had an eerie feeling, almost as if a voice was speaking to me from somewhere unknown. The hair on my arms bristled. My heart raced. A chill came over me. I told Kathy I was certain we were close to where my father was mortally wounded. His outfit had been in combat just four days and had managed to move only seven miles against the stout German Panzer forces and their natural accomplices, the hedgerows. The casualty toll was unbelievably heavy—more than one thousand men per mile dead or wounded. We visited other D-Day landmarks as well. There was a stop at Ste. Mere Eglise, the first town liberated by US paratroopers, technically the night before the actual invasion; it also was the temporary burial place for my dad and fourteen thousand other Americans before the Omaha Beach cemetery was ready in 1949. An American ex-pat, Phillipe Jutras, guided us through the Airborne Museum that he headed there and showed us other local landmarks.

Then onto Pointe du Hoc, the towering German gun emplacement that was overtaken on D-Day by a small band of fearless, cliff-scaling US Rangers, and other than the cemetery perhaps the most recognizable of all the invasion landmarks. Finally, east to Aromanches, midpoint of Gold Beach, the first of three invaded by the British and Canadian forces and site of the ingenious artificial Mulberry Ports invented by the English to facilitate the landings; some of those are still visible.

As cathartic and fulfilling as it was, the Normandy trip did not completely slake my thirst for information about my father. Rivers, the cemetery superintendent, gave me the name of a local self-educated expert on the invasion and the fighting that ensued in Normandy during the summer of 1944. His name was Henri Lefauvre. He lived in Perriers and worked as an easement official for the local utility. As such, he was familiar with every section of land in the vicinity. After several months of back and forth correspondence, one day I received a package from Monsieur Lefauvre. From his extensive sources, he plotted the movement of the 330th regiment and its whereabouts July 8. An enclosed map bore a crimson magic marker triangle indicating within plus or minus four hundred yards the spot where my father fell. Lefauvre apologized that he could not be more accurate than that; his map confirmed that the paranormal sensations I was having near the junction of those country roads in the hedgerows was *not* coincidental. I'd been standing almost dead center within Lefauvre's 400-yard margin of error! I wrote him back to convey the news, to express my gratitude, and to say his apology was *not* accepted. It was unnecessary. God had been at work through him.

Then I discovered an Eighty-Third Infantry Association, a sort of divisional alumni group. I asked the head of the organization if I could try to locate any surviving members who may have known my father, served with him, or had been there when he was killed. My request was published as an item in their newsletter.

Several months passed and I'd almost forgotten about the newsletter item when one weekday Kathy got a phone call at home from the wife of a veteran from Fort Wayne, Indiana, who became too emotional to speak with me upon reading my query. She said her husband would call me personally later after he'd collected himself. That evening he called. He'd been an enlisted man serving under Lieutenant Finnigan. He remembered when my father was hit and how it affected the men in his company. "Your dad was a good guy, a fair-minded leader who really cared about his men," the old gentleman said. By then I was just as interested in knowing what kind of a man and soldier my father was as much as the circumstances of his death.

Two weeks later another World War II veteran called. He was from the Blue Ridge high country of North Carolina, and his accent was so thick I had to ask him to repeat himself often during the conversation. He too had served under my dad and was nearby when the incoming fire hit. Joe Sr. and his radioman died instantly, the man recalled. "I don't know what it was—either a mortar shell or a fragment from an eighty-eight millimeter cannon. It was terrible. We lost so many good people, and your dad was one of the best," he added.

After a lifetime of knowing and feeling so little of my father, that piece of my life opened up in a manner beyond my wildest imagination. It must have been divine ordination, I thought, given the circumstances: my friend from Virginia calling and sending the photos after happening upon Joe Sr.'s grave; the chance meeting with the cemetery superintendent and the information he shared; the flowers at the grave; the inexplicable sensations that came over me at the junction of those rural roads in the hedgerows; connecting with Henri Lefauvre and his confirming information; and finally the calls from the men who knew my dad and were there when he died.

At last, I felt I could mourn his loss and that I finally had permission to quit resenting and start loving my father—World War II casualty and personal hero.

Patricia O'Malley was a year old when her father, Richard, a major with the Twelfth infantry, was killed by a sniper in Normandy. Later in life she wrote of seeing his headstone upon her first visit to the American Cemetery at Omaha Beach. "I cried for the joy of being there and the sadness of my father's death. I cried for all the times I needed a father and never had one. I cried for all the words I wanted to say and wanted to hear but had not. I cried and cried." Her words, another quote pulled from Atkinson's The Guns at Last Light, *conveyed my first visit feelings perfectly.*

Seventy-One

US aerospace big dogs—Boeing, North American Rockwell, Northrup Grumman, and Lockheed Martin—plus some smaller contractors and fringe-clinging special interest groups all joined forces to invite a number of major public relations agencies to submit ideas for a campaign promoting the benefits of space exploration to Joe and Sally Six Pack as well as the politicians who appropriate funds for the federal space agency—deciding the fate of NASA and other multibillion-dollar projects aimed at stretching the boundaries of the universe. Fleishman-Hillard was among those invited to compete for the business.

When I got the request for proposal, or RFP as it's known in agency parlance, my first call was to Jim Morice, my longtime colleague who headed the agency's public affairs practice group. "It looks like these people are pretty well financed and they're serious. NASA's budget has been sliced repeatedly in recent years, and the American public could give a rat's rear end. What say we combine forces—your issues people and my marketing communications team—and take a run at this thing?"

Equally intrigued, Morice agreed. Several weeks later F-H was one of seven agencies to descend on the Broadmoor in Colorado Springs to present their recommendations to a committee representing the participating companies. It was their task to review the proposals and select an agency.

Advocating portrayal of both the relevance and romance of space exploration—a concept conjured up by the sagacious Morice—we overwhelmed the competition and captivated the fancy of the decision makers. It called for a campaign dubbed Mission HOME, the acronym being shorthand for Harvesting Opportunities for Mother Earth, a strategic ploy stressing the myriad benefits of the space program to all Americans and, indeed, other earthlings. We launched it at the Smithsonian's National Air and Space Museum with extensive media coverage and key Congressional endorsements. Former astronaut James Lovell of Apollo 13 fame agreed to chair the campaign; he capably emceed the kickoff. Irrepressible lunar astronaut Edwin "Buzz" Aldrin also was on hand. He made some rather non sequitur remarks about the inevitability and allure of interplanetary tourism and then wandered around the fringes of the event seeking to be interviewed by anyone with a notebook or microphone.

As the Smithsonian event wound down, longtime (now former) *CBS Evening News* anchor Dan Rather made a grand, unexpected appearance and asked to interview Lovell as part of a series of vignettes with key twentieth century figures with whom the network was preparing to mark the new millennium. Lovell was committed to a number of other media obligations first, interviews that would take at least an hour, so I kept Rather at bay in a conference room as his camera crew readied their gear. Afterward, an agency colleague asked what it was like to babysit Dan Rather. "Let me put it this way," I said. "He was the only media person to show up unannounced, expecting us to drop everything so he could leapfrog all the others, and who wanted time with Lovell for an altogether different purpose. That's all I have to say about the great Dan Rather."

We designed a logo to use to symbolically authenticate products developed as a direct result of space-related science and technology, making it available free of charge to qualified applicants.

We wrote and syndicated a weekly newspaper column under Lovell's byline that ultimately appeared on a regular basis in more than 150 newspapers coast to coast. Town hall meetings bearing public witness to both the everyday and esoteric benefits of space were held in Baltimore, Chicago, Cleveland, Dallas, and other key markets. Space heroes keynoted the sessions—figures like Lovell, the enigmatic and self-absorbed Aldrin, the indefatigable shuttle veteran Charlie Walker, and others.

Mission HOME was a *qualified* success. In town hall hearings, proselytized partisans urged Congress to increase NASA's budget after several years of drastic cutbacks, and independent surveys indicated a detectable, positive turnaround in public opinion in favor of continued space exploration and related public and private investment.

Yet after just two years, regrettably, the campaign withered, succumbing to the weight of an abiding distrust between the aerospace giants who funded it and general impatience with the idea of an initiative that agency experts insisted from the outset would need at least five years to achieve any lasting effect.

Seventy-Two

The tech revolution was coming and it was coming fast. Case in point: the call I got one day from an old acquaintance from the Reagan/Olympic benefit project. The fast-talking, well-connected fellow had put together a group of investors to buy Sales Kit, a local computer software developer with a promising product geared to the IT needs of companies with large, far-flung sales forces. He wanted to raise the profile of the company and its products and thought F-H could handle it.

A couple of tech-savvy agency account executives and I met with him and mapped out a plan to achieve his objectives. "We feel quite comfortable taking this on," I told him, "but there are two provisos: first, it's assumed that your principal product is as good as you claim, because as we roll out our campaign the product will be road-tested by independent critical reviewers. Second, we'll need four to six months to reach full speed." The client said he understood and that the time frame was acceptable.

Less than eight weeks into the relationship, however, the client called to set up a meeting to introduce us to his new marketing chieftain, a fellow he'd recruited from Novell, then a high-flyer in the exploding software category. It did not go well. The new guy clearly was not excited about leaving his home in Salt Lake City, nor was he pleased about inheriting someone else's agency. He made no bones about the fact that he had his own PR people out West, and he intended to use them.

A week or so later, we were informed that Sales Kit had decided to go in that other direction for its PR needs. "After our recent meeting and the silence we've encountered from you since, we've been expecting this," I said. "It's too bad you didn't wait until you had your new guy onboard. If you'd said anything about your plans when you hired us, we'd have been able to avoid the time and money it's cost us and you—Management 101."

When the axe fell, the client was sitting on Fleishman-Hillard invoices for two month's work. The balance was not huge—less than $25,000-but sixty days later it remained unpaid. When I called to ask about the status of the past due bills, the ex-client first feigned surprise they'd not been paid. Then, about-face, he said he felt he should not have been liable for the fees in view of the brief relationship. I responded firmly: "The agency was ramping up in good faith, developing work product and targeting the contacts we'd need to implement your program. What's more, since we were in a startup mode, I wrote off several thousand dollars' worth of time before those invoices ever left our accounting department. That's all documented in the attachments. Those bills are legitimate and need to be paid." Begrudgingly, he finally said he would take care of the matter.

Yet after several more weeks there was still no payment. I called again, saying I'd be out that afternoon to pick up a check for the full amount. Again he balked. "OK, have it your way," I replied, "but you need to know we're going to have more than $25,000 worth of revenge at your expense. You'll be served with papers tomorrow advising you we've filed suit to recover what's rightly ours. We'll also be asking for untold damages, since you agreed to settle up and you're reneging on your word. At the same time we'll be using the media lists we put together to instead tell the world you're a deadbeat. And I'm personally going to hand-deliver the first copy of our legal complaint to Jerry Berger at the *Post-Dispatch*. He'll have a field day with it in his column. So have it your way, pal."

That did the trick. The erstwhile client loved the spotlight. He especially liked to see his name in Berger's gossip column. It made him feel like an honest-to-goodness player. He also had a healthy respect for the grief and embarrassment the wrong kind of exposure in that column could inflict. "There'll be a check in the full amount for you this afternoon," he said.

"Now you're coming to your senses; I'll be there at three o'clock," I promised, "and don't worry about a farewell party."

• • •

After stints as a publicist for a couple of Hollywood movie studios and for Saint Louis's Muny Opera and KMOX Radio, Jerry Berger spent decades as the well-read gossip columnist for the late, lamented *Globe-Democrat* and later the *Post-Dispatch.*

At an event I emceed once at which Berger was the featured speaker, I introduced him by saying there were two types of people in Saint Louis—those who read Berger's column religiously and those who vehemently denied they ever did. I allowed as how those in the former category were well-informed and appropriately titillated while those in the other group were damn liars. He was that big a deal in the local media scene, dishing the dirt as he did, often displaying astonishing access to the escapades and back stories of the town's most prominent and powerful people. (Over the years I was a frequent, regular, and presumably trusted contributor of content to Berger for his column, and on more than one occasion ghostwrote material for his use at various charity roasts and other public events.)

Berger notoriously put his scoops ahead of accuracy, which no doubt drove his editors crazy, and it was no secret in certain circles that he could be bought, thus guaranteeing that he would write only positive things, or nothing at all, depending, on behalf of those who did the purchasing.

Yet one Friday morning I opened the *Post-Dispatch,* turned to Berger's column, and read that a friend who held a key position with the Saint Louis office of D'Arcy, Masius, Benton & Bowles Advertising,